Pure New Covenant Grace

Confident access into the presence, power, and resources of

God through the gift of <u>His</u> righteous perfection

David Branch

Copyright 2020 by David Branch on behalf of the Salem City Trust. All rights reserved. In accordance with the U.S Copyright Act of 1976, the scanning, uploading, and electronic sharing of any part of this book without the permission of the publisher is unlawful piracy and theft of the author's intellectual property. If you would like to use material from the book for public use and personal gain, prior written permission must be obtained by contacting the publisher at David@purenewcovenantgrace.com. Thank you for your support and respect of the author's legal rights.

All scripture quotations are taken from the
King James Version of the Bible.

Created in the United States of America

Contents

Introduction	1
Forgiven Forever	**8**
The Grace of Christ	10
Our Grace Foundation	18
Partnering with God	31
God's Quid Pro Quo	36
No Shame, No More	44
Two Rules of Bible Study	51
Forgiveness is Past Tense	54
Once and For All	58
Righteousness with God	**73**
The Reward of Faith	75
Righteousness Lost & Found	82
The Model of Faith	88
Working the Works of God	95
The Primary Assignment of Holy Spirit	104
The Work of Righteousness	109
Focus on the Good Side	116
Paul's Warning to the Church	123
The End of the Law	**130**
A Tale of Two Trees	132
God's Plan A	138
Man's Plan B	146
Co-Existing Covenants	150
A People in Rebellion	155
Mutiny on the Mountain	158

Mission Impossible	164
Don't Even Touch It	172
A Final Word of Caution	190
Life After the Resurrection	198
Where Do I Go from Here?	207

Introduction

In this season, a global grace revolution is the prepared strategy of our heavenly Father, and it's already begun. Almighty God is awakening His Sons and Daughters to the gift of <u>His</u> righteousness so we can receive an abundance of <u>His</u> grace. A rediscovery of the original grace of Christ is the method by which believers will navigate through these times with unparalleled peace, strength, and confidence. Although the enemy is desperately trying to prevent this move of God, nothing can stop born again, blood-

Introduction

bought believers who are willing to consider that God is so much better than we've previously known. The simplicity of His plan is awe inspired, and of course, Jesus is the central focus. Through the clear separation of Old Covenant religion and His Pure New Covenant Grace, every believer will possess the keys to the kingdom, as our true and glorious identity in Christ is revealed. By the grace of our Savior alone; no one is disqualified or excluded.

Regardless of your past mistakes, present lifestyle and even sin that's yet to be committed, you're positioned for this grace that cannot be earned or deserved. God has chosen this time to remove the limitations of ungodly religion. He's chosen this time, to re-train our focus on Jesus and the full benefit of His work. By doing so, the gospel of the grace of Christ, the greatest power of God on earth to deliver, provide, heal and protect, will usher in a unity of "the faith" that hasn't been seen since the first century.

According to scripture, the grace of God can only flow as designed by Him, through His righteousness.

Pure New Covenant Grace Series Part One

The more we know about God's righteousness, the greater the flow of His grace. But unfortunately, righteousness has almost become a bad word. Rather than receiving it as a blessing that God can flow through, it's been commonly presented as a high moral standard that believers must comply. Most believers immediately think about the burden of having to <u>do</u> righteousness rather than the blessing of <u>being</u> righteous through faith. As a young Christian, I was often reminded that I needed to be "uncompromisingly righteous" to receive anything from God. In all my efforts of doing, grace was cut off. <u>Doing</u> for righteousness is quite literally, the opposite of the grace of Christ.

Sure, God was still merciful to this disqualified son until he was eventually awakened to the righteous perfection of Christ that was with me all along. The question of <u>how</u> righteousness is received and maintained is the billion-dollar question.

In this first of a three-part series, we're going to look at the three primary obstacles that restrict the grace of Christ. The first is the worst.

Introduction

Unbelief in the forgiveness of sins made possible by the death of Jesus at the cross, is by far, the most common disqualifier from the grace of Christ.

The forgiveness of sins is the first component of the gospel. It's the path that leads to righteousness, the Kingdom of God and every promise in which we depend. As we cry out to God, "Lord, forgive me…" we demonstrate our lack of faith in Him and the work of His Son. This faith failure is an indication that we've accepted a religious lie. To plead with God for something He's already accomplished denies the grace of Christ. Seeking more forgiveness from God to relieve our guilty conscience is a religious alternative to faith in the gospel. This is religion of the worst kind. For stability in the Kingdom of God and confidence toward Him <u>always</u>, this first component of the gospel must be settled. Jesus paid for <u>all</u> our sins; well-pleasing faith receives <u>all</u> the benefit.

The second obstacle that limits the grace of God is our inability to consistently connect with the righteous perfection of Christ. Righteousness, the second component of the gospel, is a gift we received when we accepted forgiveness for our sins in Christ. Although the gift will never be withdrawn by God, it must be continually received by faith. Every believer has been given this priceless and powerful status before God. But for the most part, since the gift of righteousness is dependent upon faith in our forgiveness, it's lying dormant, inactive and neglected.

For this powerful blessing to be effective, the righteousness of God in heaven requires an awakened vessel of righteousness in the earth, and a faith connection between the two. To see Pure New Covenant Grace rain upon us all, each of us must fight the good fight to hold on consistently to the gift of our righteous perfection in Christ. He truly did it all!

The third obstacle that restricts the grace of Christ is our flawed attempts at righteousness through our own efforts to perform religious standards. Through teaching that mistakenly blends the two covenants together, many believers are motivated by right-doing instead of right-believing. The Law and the spirit of the Law is righteousness that is works-based. There's no such thing. The scripture is quite clear; no one under

Introduction

the Law obtained righteousness with God by doing good works or performing disciplined acts of "obedience."

Attempting to keep the Law only produces failure in the lives of New Covenant believers. Seeking God's acceptance through our behavior, discipline, performance etc., etc., is a sure-fire recipe for failure. "Trying" to please God with our good works is a nullification of His grace. Pure New Covenant Grace is the supply of His resources that enable our performance, not a burden placed on our backs. In these pages, you're not going to find the many things that you must <u>do</u> to be righteous. But rather, all that Jesus has already <u>done</u> on your behalf.

Pure New Covenant Grace is divided into these three foundational sections that will help you to hear from the Lord more clearly in these times when He's needed most. When you read something that strikes you significantly, please stop and prayerfully consider what the Lord is saying to you. Look up scriptures as Holy Spirit leads. Allow the ebb and flow of His presence to be a gentle reminder to embrace the path that you're on. It's not important how fast you get through this work, but rather, how much gets in you.

As your load gets lighter and your path gets brighter, please send a Pure New Covenant Grace online link to your friends and family. All of us have an especially important part to play in His global grace revolution. I genuinely believe that every believer worldwide will begin to experience Him like never before, as we receive the abundance of His unearned, unmerited favor and the gift of His righteous perfection. Thank you and enjoy!

Forgiven Forever

Pure New Covenant Grace Series Part One

The Grace of Christ

The best definition for grace is the unearned, unmerited, and undeserved favor of God. The greatest expression of Gods Pure Grace is Jesus Himself. He's the person of grace that we haven't earned and don't deserve. So much more than a cloak for sin as some might think; every resource, provision and supernatural gifting comes from Him by His grace. So much more than a message or a movement, the grace of God is His part of our mutual covenant, assured by the blood of Jesus. Grace, before and after the cross is the method by which God has been able to exert His influence in the earth. Since the sin of Adam in the garden, no one qualifies or deserves the overflowing goodness of God. But, since the work of Jesus at the cross, everyone has access.

According to scripture, we can be strong in the grace of Christ or weak. We can receive an abundance of grace or just a trickle. The strength and the quantity of the supply of His grace is dependent upon our faith in the person of Grace and the work that He came to complete. The good news for us all, by definition, grace is not dependent upon our behavior, discipline, or ability. The apostle Paul shares:

> *"For by grace are ye saved through faith; and that not of yourselves: it is the <u>gift</u> of God: <u>Not of works</u>, lest any man should boast."*
> Ephesians 2:8, 9

Everything that we receive from God comes this way, by grace through faith. The pure grace of Christ saves us from lack, sickness, despair, depression, stress, guilt, addiction, loneliness... whatever we need saving from, and yet, without our works.

The Grace of Christ, The Faith, The Grace of God, The Gospel of Grace, The New Covenant and The New Testament, are all describing the same thing that began with the cross. The unearned, unmerited and undeserved favor of God is the common theme in each of these biblical references. They all point to Jesus, the facilitator of the grace of God to bless an undeserving people. <u>Only</u> by grace can our heavenly Father bless people that have been disqualified by the nature of sin. What grace tells every "believer," again, by definition, you are well-equipped to receive from Him. No one is left out because the focus of the Father is not on you, but the Christ in you.

Accompanying the person of grace, there's another blessing that must be received for God to have maximum expression in our lives; that is, the gift of <u>His</u> righteousness. Righteousness with God is a far reaching, supernatural gifting, blessing and power that enables man to fellowship and commune with the power source of all life.

There are only two people in the history of the world that enjoyed a pure and tangible righteousness with God, the first man created in the image and likeness of God, and Jesus, the firstborn Son of God Himself. In the garden of Eden, Adam and his creator had clear communication with each other, as God made every provision for his new life. Adam was naked, unashamed, and unafraid as he lived in continuous fellowship with God, prior to His disobedience. Through their partnership, God could flow freely and unhindered in the earth, as He pleased.

Scripture doesn't tell us how long Adam enjoyed his privileged existence with God before His error, but we know the glory of his righteous purity was lost. The righteous connection between God and Adam was broken. With Adam's own righteousness gone forever, God would now have to re-establish righteousness with man if He was ever to have influence in the earth again.

Since Adam's disobedience until today, the restoration plan is revealed in what the scripture calls, the righteousness of God "by faith." Although not as tangible as Adam's righteousness before his failure, this righteousness is disbursed by faith in the Righteous One. Faith in the lamb slain from the foundation of the world allows God to continue to supply His power and resources to impact our lives with His goodness. Despite Adam's failure, God's been able to carry out His plan to save, protect and bless to the extent that we believe in Him.

Throughout bible history, righteousness by faith can be found in the lives of everyone that's accomplished anything great in partnership with God. From Abel, Enoch, Noah and Abraham; to Daniel, Samson, Gideon and King David, all received the righteousness of God by faith.

Jesus, on the other hand, was born in absolute righteous perfection. Without the sin-stained blood of Adam coursing through His veins, Jesus became acutely aware of His righteous status. Understanding this righteousness afforded Him access to His heavenly Father like no other. He's the best example of what a relationship between a righteous God and a righteous man should be. He was confident the Father would supply his every need with Kingdom resources of power, provision and protection. He knew how to follow His Father; doing what He was shown and speaking what He heard. The fellowship between them was consistent and reliable. Since Jesus died in the position of perfect righteousness with God, His righteous status is permanently sealed for all of eternity. Through Jesus, we're partakers of His eternal righteousness as a <u>gift</u> of our salvation. That's right, you are the righteousness of God in Christ, forever!

Grace and the gift of His righteousness work hand in hand. In fact, according to Paul in his letter to the Romans, we can see God's recipe for winning in life.

"For if by one man's offence death reigned by one; much more they which receive <u>abundance</u> of grace and of the <u>gift</u> of righteousness shall reign in life by one, Jesus Christ." Romans 5:17

The word "receive" here is translated from the Greek word that means: "to take, to lay hold of, to carry away, to claim for oneself." The abundance of His grace <u>and</u> the gift of His righteousness both, must be "taken" and embraced. The task before every believer is to open the package that contains this gift and take it, again and again. The more we know, the more we can take.

By providing the full supply of His grace and the gift of His righteousness through Jesus, God is keeping His Word and fulfilling every promise of scripture. Paul sheds more light in his letter to the Romans of the relationship between grace and His righteousness.

> *"That as sin hath reigned unto death, even so might grace reign <u>through</u> righteousness unto eternal life by Jesus Christ our Lord."*
> Romans 5:21

Imagine a conduit or channel that connects the righteousness of God in heaven with His righteousness in you, here on earth. Now imagine God's power, wisdom and all the resources of His Kingdom descending into your life through this channel of His righteousness. Your faith in Jesus and His righteous perfection in you, draws the desires of your heart and all things needful, by the unearned, undeserved, and unmerited favor of God. The reward for taking by faith the abundance of His grace and the gift of His righteousness is a life of rest and peace, as the unforced rhythms of grace goes before us and prospers our way. The measure and strength of the grace of Christ to radically transform our lives is dependent first, upon our faith in the work of Jesus at the cross. And unfortunately, this perfect work has been imperfectly represented. The first obstacle that stands tall, loud, and proud in our way, is unbelief in the <u>fullness</u> of the forgiveness of sins through Christ.

From online survey questionnaires in North America, it appears that upwards of 80% of those professing to be born again believers stumble at this first faith hurdle. If the rest of the world is having as much trouble believing this scripturally sound first benefit of the gospel, we're truly in the beginnings of a global grace revolution.

Once the walls of this first obstacle come down, all the others are coming down as well. Like the most meticulously designed dominoes structure, walls that uphold unscriptural religious traditions, and those that limit access to the promises of God, are all coming down.

Our Grace Foundation

"...Ye are God's building. According to the grace of God, which is given unto me, as a wise master builder, I have laid the foundation, and another builds thereon. But let every man take heed how he builds thereupon. For other foundation can no man lay than that is laid, which is Jesus Christ."
1 Corinthians 3:9-11

The building of our spiritual house of faith begins with the Chief Cornerstone, the Rock of our salvation and the anchor of our soul. In fact, the plan of God for every believer in the process of building a personal, spiritual temple that houses the presence of God, not one brick should be added on top of another until the foundation is established. Who Jesus is and what He accomplished for us, is the foundation that upholds all the promises of God. Jesus is the author and the finisher of ALL faith.

Before the earth was created; the sun, moon and stars formed, and before God ever said, "Let there be light," Jesus is the lamb slain before the foundation of the world. Before any ink was put to parchment to reveal the promises that are assured us in scripture, God set a specific moment in time to offer of Himself, a brutal, merciless sacrifice for the <u>sin</u> of Adam and the <u>sins</u> of all mankind. Faith today, right now in fact, in the tangible, scriptural & historical real-life events of over 2,000 years ago is the catalyst that connects us to "the exceeding great and precious promises," described by Peter. Before you were even a twinkle in your natural daddy's eye, He's the solution before you knew you had a problem. Before your many so-called disobediences and failures, your name was written in His book, you were set apart, and granted eternal life with Him. Faith in this finished work of Grace by Christ, is the gospel that cannot be earned or deserved.

By the grace of God alone, whether it was last week or decades ago, God sent someone to share with us a story of the grace of Christ. The Holy Spirit was already involved and began to stir up the faith that God placed on the inside of us all. We knew we were hearing the truth; that Jesus paid the inescapable penalty for our sin at the cross and was resurrected on the third day. We probably didn't know anything about doctrine, an inheritance, authority, or covenants. What we were accurately told is that salvation was free and came by simply accepting the resurrected one who offered up His life on our behalf. On that day, we responded to His grace and invited the risen Christ into our heart and life. From that moment, we were "born again" into the family of God that began with the firstborn Son.

Our salvation through Christ was the first building block of faith, which originated and was initiated by grace. Our part was quite simple. All that God required for His grace to operate at peak efficiency was our agreement. He didn't ask for our time, our service or money. He didn't ask us to quit smoking, drinking, or cussing. All that was necessary to begin living a presently blessed life with an eternally perfect gift of righteousness, was to believe and confess what He had already said and done. At that precise moment, God Himself made His home on the inside of us. Despite the many flaws in our hearts and our lives that would soon show up again (possibly later that same day), God qualified us through His perfect gift.

Unfortunately, like a brand-new computer with unlimited storage, we began to download from both, trusted and untrusted sources. Consider for a moment how many people have shaped our belief since that first day of our salvation. Family members and friends; out-of-season pastors, preachers on TV and radio, and random strangers on social media, all uploading truth, half-truths, bits and pieces of truth, and downright foolishness. How many churches have you visited that will never be graced with your presence again, and for good reason? Have you ever attended a funeral where someone said that God "took" a loved one because He wanted another flower in His garden? Have you heard that sin breaks the fellowship with God, but not the relationship? Everything that we've received along our journey has shaped our view and opinion of God. How we see Him, and just as important, how we see Him as He's looking at us, determines the quality and boundaries of our relationship.

Somehow, the great majority of believers have exchanged what began as a free, blessed and hopeful relationship of love and generosity, into a laborious, guilt-laden work that produces minimal results. But as we re-focus our eyes on Jesus and His work at the cross, it's enough to transform every heart and loose the weight of every burden.

As we see Him accurately, without the Old Covenant additives of works-based righteousness, and truly embrace the same grace of God that began this incredible journey, the person of grace will gain access to every area of our lives.

One prominent misconception that must be addressed here is the false idea that faith begins where the will of God is known. This flawed doctrine, which is commonly presented to believers, embraces the notion that faith is produced by finding promises in scripture that address a point of need. Then, believers should begin prayerfully meditating and exercising faith for that promise, expecting God's best. This is the path of the great majority of Christianity, but clearly not the beginning of faith. The reason this concept is dangerous, much like the secular version of this found in the law of attraction, is because believers are seeking the benefits of the Kingdom without the consent of the King. In other words, the much weightier matter of the gospel is neglected in this equation.

Faith for the New Covenant believer for anything promised by God still begins with Jesus at the cross, or it's not faith at all. Let's look at a verse of scripture that's familiar to many regarding faith. From the book of Hebrews Chapter 11:1, we see a great description of faith, followed by great men and women of God, who used this faith to accomplish great results.

> *"Now faith is the substance of things hoped for, the evidence of things not seen."*

This verse presents a doctrinal truth concerning faith that has been woefully neglected. Is it possible to have a defining verse of scripture concerning faith, without an emphasis on Christ and His finished work? The clear answer is no. As Christ Himself said, "without me you can do nothing." If we look beyond the surface of this text in Hebrews, we can see that Jesus, and the work that He finished at the cross is the centerpiece of all faith. Let's take this verse and separate it into two parts. On the one hand, we see that faith is both <u>substance and evidence</u>. Substance and evidence can be both handled and seen. Remember 1 John 1:1-3?

> *"That which was from the beginning, which we have heard, which we have seen with our eyes, which we have looked upon, and our hands have handled, of the Word of life: (For the life was manifested, and we have seen it, and bear witness, and shew unto you that eternal life, which was with the Father, and was manifested unto us;) that which we have seen and heard declare we unto you, that ye also may have fellowship with us: and truly our fellowship is with the Father, and with His Son Jesus Christ."*

And for the purpose of adding a 2nd witness, let's also look at 2nd Peter 1:16

> *"For we have not followed cunningly devised fables, when we made known unto you the power and coming of our Lord Jesus Christ but were eyewitnesses of His majesty."*

The broken body and spilled blood of our Savior is the tangible <u>substance</u> of faith, based upon an actual event that has already taken place in the torturous death of Jesus. His blood should be our daily reminder that we've already received forgiveness for ALL our sins, including every disobedience and failure. The <u>evidence</u>, or proof of our faith, that the transaction of our sins, in exchange for His righteousness, is conclusively expressed in the resurrection of Christ.

With every inspired, heart-filled tear in worship, with every revelation received from the throne of grace, every well-timed comfort or joy, and so much more, is Holy Spirit bearing witness that our redemption is complete. Although Jesus is the lamb slain from the foundation of the world, it was at these specific moments in human history that these two very real events took place. By the substance and evidence of our faith in His work, we are holy, righteous, and redeemed, each and every day of our lives. Both components of the gospel together, the death and the resurrection, is the power of God that we must continually establish. Our grasp of these events and these specific benefits that have been secured by Christ, will determine how well we flow in agreement with the Lord.

On the other hand, the <u>things hoped for,</u> and <u>things not seen</u>, are the many intangible promises of God, from Genesis, the book of beginnings to the Revelation of John. The substance and evidence that is received and active is our source of power that makes the secondary promises of God possible.

So far, in defining our faith, we've made a distinction between the work of the cross and the promises of God. Let's now dive a little deeper along these same lines and make a further distinction between the substance and evidence, the two components that comprise the foundation of our faith.

On the day of His death, the forgiveness of sins for everyone in the world throughout history was complete. God sent an open invitation of redemption from Adam's sin, and forgiveness of our own, to the entire world. Your acceptance of that invitation has secured your place at the table, and in the family of God.

The penalties for our past, present and future sins have all been satisfied once and forever as if the sin never took place. God, without the restraints of time and space, has made the decree of your forgiveness abundantly clear throughout the scriptures. Regardless of what religion has proposed as a compromise to this truth, this is the starting point of all New Covenant faith and every scriptural promise.

You're forgiven now and forever of every thought, word or deed. Every failure of behavior, performance, discipline and will-power have already been forgiven. Use your imagination how far forgiveness from "all" transgressions can go, and then go further. How far is the East from the West? It never stops. Neither has God in separating you from your sins.

Forgiven Forever

Ask yourself the question, is my failure greater than the intentionally spilled blood of God-in-the-flesh? Of course not, regardless the transgression.

The forgiveness of sins is the faith point of entry that leads to all the blessing, reward and benefits that are promised to the righteous. As we hold fast to the truth of our forgiveness in Christ, we gain access into every other door within the Kingdom of God. The overwhelming blessing and benefit that we receive for aligning the thoughts of our mind in agreement with the settled truth and reality of our spirit, on this issue, the forgiveness of sins, is progressive peace and stability with God. Guilt, insecurity, stress, worry, sin and condemnation all dissipate into nothing as we live with an awareness of our forgiveness from God in Christ. Though religion may consider this to be a small thing. I assure you it's not. Without the embrace of your full forgiveness, the door of doubt and unbelief remains wide open.

Unbelief in this one thing invites instability in everything. This can be a matter of life and death. There's no room for doubt when sickness or disease comes our way. In fact, the sacrament of Holy Communion is the method that God has chosen to put us in remembrance of these truths for our healing and strength. We are instructed by Jesus Himself, as recorded by Matthew, Mark, Luke, John and Paul, to discern His broken body and the blood that made the forgiveness of sins possible. It's the remembrance of the details that draws healing in our body. Our power to rise above every situation begins with this first aspect of the gospel.

For the body of Christ at large to be the glorious church, without spot or wrinkle, holy and without blemish, the religious and unscriptural crutch of seeking God's forgiveness under the guise of Old Covenant repentance, must be removed. This is only possible through the faith that Abraham demonstrated, "who considered not his body now dead."

Unbelief in our New Covenant, fear of judgement, guilt and condemnation, all prevent believers from taking hold of the promises that are much needed now. Through the cloud of religion, the substance and evidence aren't being embraced by more than 80% of the church. The practice of seeking forgiveness from God for something He's told us is not only forgiven but never to be imputed again, rather than appropriating faith in His finished work, is the most common religious and unscriptural approach to dealing with sin. It's impossible to stand in faith, both guilty and forgiven at the same time. It's impossible for both, you and Jesus to be guilty of the same crime. We have been given these great and precious promises to rise above every challenge that we face without fail. But just as the death of Jesus comes before His resurrection, so too must the acceptance of the forgiveness of sins precede the gift and benefits of His righteous perfection in you.

Pure New Covenant Grace Series Part One

Partnering with God

God has always dealt with man through the terms of a covenant agreement. By necessity, God in heaven, must have a partner on earth that He can work through to accomplish His desire here. In scripture, we see covenants with Adam, Noah, the promises to Abraham, the Law of Moses and the New Covenant established by Jesus. Each of these covenants had specific terms and varying responsibilities. Every prior covenant arrangement between God and man was designed to get us to this point in history. The New Covenant is the most important of all because this covenant will usher in the appearing and 2nd coming of Christ. The end-times glorious church is ready to be revealed, and your role is vitally important.

Much like the well-known promises made to Abraham, the Patriarch of Bible faith, God has shared several promises to the New Covenant believer, that seemingly require nothing for us to do. These promises are the terms of our covenant that determine the degree of God's involvement in our lives. The young prophet Jeremiah, in Ch 31:31-34 shares:

> *"Behold, the days come, saith the Lord, that I will make a new covenant with the house of Israel, and with the house of Judah: <u>Not</u> according to the covenant that I made with their fathers in the day that I took them by the hand to bring them out of the land of Egypt; which my covenant they brake, although I was an husband unto them, saith the Lord: But this shall be the covenant that I will make with the house of Israel; After those days, saith the Lord, I will put my law in their inward parts, and write it in their hearts; and will be their God, and they shall be my people. And they shall teach no more every man his neighbor, and every man his brother, saying, Know the Lord: for they shall all know me, from the least of them unto the greatest of them, saith the Lord: <u>for I will forgive their iniquity, and I will remember their sin no more</u>."*

For God to be our deliverer, our healer, provider and protector, we have a divine mandate from heaven that's revealed in this last line. In this New Covenant, God <u>requires</u> faith that our sin has been forgiven <u>and</u> forgotten. Of the two components that make up the gospel or good news that Jesus came to bring, this is the first. You are forgiven. Every sin, whether intentional or not, is forgiven and forgotten by God. Sin that takes place in your mind, in your words and in the things that you do, have all been forgiven. It may have only been a few years ago that you accepted Jesus as your Savior from sin, but that was not when you were forgiven. God forgave you, and everyone else on the planet, over 2,000 years ago. However, to be of any present benefit to the saint or the sinner, His grace should be received as if He just gave His life today.

Beyond anything that can be imagined, our heavenly Father desires that we live in unbroken fellowship with Him. It's one thing to receive assurances of His forgiveness from time to time in our devotions, and on Sundays when the choir is especially tuned in. It's a different thing altogether, to live in that same peace, assurance and confidence toward God daily. It's not enough that God alone, from where He dwells outside the realm of time, has declared your eternal forgiveness. Our Father is looking for this benefit of the cross to be received daily by His children; the just shall <u>live</u> by faith.

Do you believe that you're forgiven by God today? Do you believe that the forgiveness of your sins is a finished work? Are you eternally righteous before God, regardless of the errors committed in your flesh? These are truly important questions that help us locate our faith in Christ. Every Christian believed the gospel at one time; this is how we became born again.

Salvation was purely a work by grace through faith. However, over the course of time, religion and religious tradition made us question the simplicity of the gospel. We began to work for something that was once offered freely. We began to ask, again and again, for something that we already have.

Jesus asked a curious question to His disciples saying:

> *"...When the Son of man cometh, shall he find faith on the earth? Luke 18:8*

In His question here, the Lord is not referring to faith for a new car, house or even our healing. He's referring to faith in the terms of this New Covenant, the gospel of the Grace of Christ. When the Son of Man returns, will He find Christians that have embraced the glorious position of righteousness in Him through the forgiveness of sins? Jesus alone is the judge of our faith. He's the one who determines if agreement in our covenant has been accomplished.

Are you seeking His forgiveness every time you fail? Are you accepted by God at sometimes more than others? Is God pleased with you on the days that you do well, but not so much when you err? Are you confident in your relationship with God by faith in His righteousness or in your righteous efforts? Faith that pleases God is faith in the work of His Son.

Today, without fear, judgment or condemnation, let's prove together the strength of our good news, as we separate ourselves from the unscriptural religious traditions of the past.

God's Quid Pro Quo

"*Be it known unto you therefore, men and brethren, that through this man is preached unto you the <u>forgiveness of sins</u>: And by Him all that believe (in the forgiveness of sins) are <u>justified</u> from all things, from which you could not be justified by the law of Moses." Acts 13:38, 39*

From the only recorded sermon that the Apostle Paul preached, this is the culmination of that message to the church at Antioch. Paul was the disciple that was entrusted with unveiling the details of the gospel of Christ, after Jesus' resurrection. This is the climactic conclusion of what the apostle Paul called "my gospel."

Notice above, that the forgiveness of sins is the primary message that's being preached. Justification, aka righteousness with God, is the <u>conditional</u> benefit of believing in the forgiveness of sins. Paul is instructing the church...

God is no longer holding anything against you...*if you believe that you're forgiven.*

There's no barrier of sin between you and God anymore...*if you believe that you're forgiven.*

There's no curse that can't be broken... *if you believe that you're forgiven.*

Righteousness with God is a gift to you... *if you believe that you're forgiven.*

All the promises of God in Christ, are yes, and in Him, Amen... *if you believe that you're forgiven.*

The forgiveness of sins by Christ is the way and the truth that leads to a life of righteousness and peace with God, as well as every other scriptural promise to "the righteous."

As mentioned, the body of Christ at large has great difficulty with this first component of the gospel. The overwhelming majority actively deny the truth of our forgiveness. Untold millions of Christians reach out to priests to confess their sins for the explicit purpose of receiving His forgiveness. Others take pride that they can share their unbelief directly to God in prayer. Some say: "Forgive me Lord for my sins of omission and sins of commission." These, as we've had explained to us from pulpits, are good things that we knew to do but didn't, and things that we shouldn't have done, but did anyway. Many of us by habit, in jest or by what the scripture calls an "evil conscience," seek forgiveness from sins that we're not even aware of. And the worst-case scenario is expressed annually among those that flog their own backs with whips and chains, spilling their blood in the streets. As if this act of penance, shedding guilty blood is greater than the pure, faultless blood of our Savior. These religious "works" are all in error because the work of Christ, from His own lips, is finished. This breach of faith is also a violation of our covenant.

Our unbelief restricts God's interventions of grace in our lives. The promises of God can never be sure when we doubt the very thing that made them possible.

The word "justified" in this text means an absolution from all guilt and punishment. The believer is justified (not guilty, absolved) before God because we've been redeemed (purchased from the debt of sin and free from its <u>spiritual</u> consequences). So, you're legally and <u>righteously</u> accepted by your heavenly Father for no other reason than you believe on the first begotten Son. Honoring the Son and His work, honors the Father.

Being "justified from all things" reflects a not-guilty verdict for every statute, ordinance, law and commandment under the Old Covenant. As many believers are aware, righteousness with God under the Law of Moses was never possible by doing good works or avoiding bad works. There's nothing then or now, that we can <u>do</u> to be righteous with God.

<u>Trying</u> and <u>doing</u> for righteousness is the enemy of righteousness. How unstable would our salvation be, if every time we failed, we lost favor with God, became displeasing to Him and forfeited our gifted position of righteousness? How weak is the cross to be considered if our faith is based on the cooperation of our flesh

rather than the shed blood of our eternal Savior? No, faith is based on the work of Jesus alone and our part is to believe we're forgiven and righteous, despite the works of the flesh.

For years, decades even, I attempted to qualify myself for His righteousness. I worked harder than anyone I knew. I served, tithed, prayed, studied, and heard what I thought was the gospel. And yet, I lived with frequent guilt and condemnation. It didn't matter how prudent my life and lifestyle were, righteousness wasn't "working" in my life. I thought that my bouts of suffering under one thing or another was a necessary part of "carrying my cross." Little did I know that living with confidence toward God daily, was not only possible, but His original plan.

Unfortunately, this message that Paul preached is not often repeated without a counterbalance. The majority will agree and disagree in the same message from week to week. Church members are encouraged to embrace their forgiveness from God, then the weight of sin-laden congregants will begin to lift. But often in the same service, the people are incorrectly warned that sin will shut off fellowship with God, and <u>you</u> have to make things right. Then you're told: "If you confess your sins to God, He's faithful and just to forgive you and to cleanse you of all unrighteousness." As we'll soon see, this scripture from 1 John 1:9 is a beautiful truth for <u>unbelievers</u> that's been misapplied so often to Christians that it's become a routine practice of unbelief.

God has already shown Himself faithful to forgive you as you acknowledged the work of His Son. He's already shown Himself to be just, which is to say, adhering to perfect justice. Since your sins were placed on Jesus, and the price for those sins paid by Him, it's just for God to attribute the identical righteousness of Christ to you. In Part two of this series, I will provide a minimum of twelve reasons why 1 John 1:9 is not addressing the New Covenant believer. Paul concluded his defining message of the gospel in his message at Antioch, with a prophetic word of warning:

> *"Beware therefore, lest that come upon you, which is spoken of in the prophets; Behold, ye despisers, and wonder, and perish: for <u>I</u> <u>work</u> a <u>work</u> in your days, a <u>work</u> which ye shall in no*

wise believe, though a man declare it unto you."
Acts 13:40, 41

If you believe that you have need of more forgiveness from God, you will continue to disqualify yourself from the benefits of righteousness through your unbelief in our covenant. As you can see, I've underscored this word "work" three times. Our heavenly Father is clearly telling us that the work of righteousness is not ours, it's His alone. Our only contribution to His finished work at the cross is our faith in His work. Paul is quoting here from Habakkuk. This warning is not a threat of eternal demise, but a word of caution to avoid neglecting the primary thing that Jesus accomplished for us.

As we take the benefit of our justification completely, God is then able to make us completely whole. By removing the religious crutch of seeking His forgiveness for our failures, and fully embrace the blood covenant, all the limitations that have prevented the full manifestation of the sons of God will also be removed. Seeing Jesus more clearly, loving Him more fully and worshiping Him more deeply is the direction that we're heading. Our heavenly Father has our freedom from sin and all its effects on His present agenda.

This gospel that Paul preached to the people of Antioch on that day was such a hopeful blessing, and unlike anything they'd heard before, they pleaded with Paul that he would preach the exact same message the following week. To this, the Apostle Paul agreed. The news of his scheduled sermon with this revolutionary concept of freedom by grace through faith, spread like wildfire.

> *"And the next sabbath day came almost the whole city together to hear the word of God."*
> Acts 13:44

No Shame, No More

Today, I imagined a huge, hardwood door that leads to a spacious house with windows all around. As I sneak a peek inside, I can see so much activity and commotion. But the only entrance is this big front door. There are teams of leaders, with their backs against the door, like suited guards, angrily fighting against crowds of people desperately trying to get inside. Only the most diligent gain entry. As I steal a glance through one of the windows, I can see men, women and children receiving healing with joy-filled eyes and tears running down their faces.

I can see people coming out of addictions as their bodies are reinvigorated to health. People with all types of sickness and disease beyond the capabilities of doctors are healed with ease. Everyone in the house is delivered and set free from all that has prevented their strength and wholeness. Everyone is joyful; smiling, wonderfully blessed and alive. In the midst of this blissful scene, elevated slightly, shining radiantly, with a smile on His face too... I see Jesus.

After this blissfully miraculous scene, I realize that I'm still on the outside looking in, and I'm reminded of the words of Jesus to the religionists of His day, the keepers of the Old Covenant of Law:

"Woe unto you, lawyers! for ye have taken away the key of knowledge: ye entered not in yourselves, and them that were entering in ye hindered." Luke 11:52

There are many in church leadership that think grace is simply a teaching, rather than a person and a covenant. They think that grace should be limited, contained and controlled. They believe that too much grace will promote debauchery and hedonism in the lives of their congregants.

Rather than trust that Jesus knows whereof He speaks, and fully preach this gospel, many are either scared of the consequences of failed leadership or steeped in unbelief themselves.

On the contrary ladies and gentlemen, grace is a person and the central focus of the New Covenant we receive by faith. Reigning in life, as we've seen, only happens by receiving a literal, super-abundance of grace. Getting to know Jesus better does not stir up carnal desires to sin. Learning about our covenant, the grace of God, is not a trap of the devil. Is there such a thing as too much Jesus???

Never-the-less, whenever grace is the topic of discussion, the religionists come out in full force to "protect" believers from an over-abundance of Jesus. Typically, they pull out their go-to scripture in the Romans 6 warning from Paul: "Shall we continue in sin, that grace may abound?" To which the voices of the global body of Christ, heard from around the world in uncanny unison, all shout out in agreement with a resounding... "NO!" Of course, not. The concept that sin is bad is common knowledge among us. This one word of caution does not excuse anyone from delivering the full gospel of His grace. Remember, it was also Paul who took the following bold stance to defend this New Covenant good news:

> *"For I am not ashamed of the gospel of Christ: for it is the power of God unto salvation to everyone that believeth..."* Romans 1:16

When the gospel of Christ is taught, without the religious strings of unbelief attached, the harnessed power of God is released in the lives of all that believe. This word "power" from the original Greek is defined as force, especially miraculous, strength, ability, abundance and might. We don't have to look any further for His power here on earth. It's in this gospel.

Power to overcome sin, lay hands on the sick, receive from His supply and overcome every obstacle is all contained within the components of the grace of Christ, The Gospel. This is the means by which God exerts His dynamic influence in the earth. The gospel encourages us to step out in faith; it helps us to receive His abundant supply, it demonstrates how to operate in might beyond our natural strength and ability, and it reveals the power of resources that arises from our association with other believers. This is all confined within these two seemingly small words, "the gospel."

The word salvation here, also from the original Greek, is defined as: "deliverance, safety and preservation." This explosive power of God is "<u>unto</u> salvation;" meaning, it's always en route somewhere. Through faith in the gospel, it's headed your way to deliver you, provide for you, to keep and protect you. Paul, who defined the gospel this way to the church at Rome, also describes this same word "power' to the church at Ephesus, as being active on the inside of us:

> *"Now unto Him that is able to do exceeding abundantly above all that we ask or think, <u>according to the power</u> that <u>worketh</u> in us..."*
> Ephesians 3:20

God is able to move in big, miraculous ways, beyond the limits of our imagination, according to how much of this gospel we <u>actively</u> receive. There's a sea of power in the grace of God that we've yet to experience. There's grace in His death and grace in His resurrection that have yet to be explored.

The benefits obtained for us in His death are too numerous to count. And the benefits of His righteousness is the gift that keeps on giving. How much? That's dependent upon our willingness to hunger and thirst after it. A full embrace of the forgiveness of sins, is the door of entry in our explorations.

The righteousness of God is more than a dormant, stagnant "position," but rather, an active spiritual resource. Notice the word "worketh." The "power that worketh in us" is the gift of His righteousness. Is the gospel something that we believe once and then put on a shelf? Not if we want effectual, working power. The inexhaustible power of God should be an active, vibrant source, to produce active, vibrant, and supernatural results.

The much, much, much more than we can ask, or think is within reach, to the extent that we see ourselves righteously qualified by the works of Christ alone. Living our lives connected daily to His righteous perfection allows Him to release His goodness, as He desires, and in His timing.

Forgiven Forever

When our failures and guilt cause us to take our eyes away from Jesus and His finished work, we disconnect from our power source. Not from Jesus or our eternal salvation ever, in any way. But we disconnect from the resources that can only be accessed by faith in the gospel. A believer that suffers from perpetual stress and anxiety is unplugging from the power. Believers that struggle with incessant hopelessness, despair and other works of the devil are living disconnected from the greatest power of God on earth.

To overcome every obstacle and live a victorious life, we only need to stay plugged-in to our power source, the grace of Christ, the power of God unto salvation. We're the righteousness of God in Christ; we're forgiven of all our sin for all time. We are His greatly beloved! Regardless of what it looks like naturally, we know who and whose we are.

Two Rules of Bible Study

Before we go further, please allow me to remind you of two very important rules of Bible study. The first and most important rule for studying scripture is that the Bible interprets the Bible. No one should ever rely upon someone else's interpretation of scripture. You could, like me, find yourself believing unintentional deceptions for most of your life, making null and void the promises of God. Even the illustrations and examples that are used by Bible teachers to help us understand scripture should be studiously scrutinized. I had a Pastor (I would never say their name) who reminded the congregants for years not to trust what anyone spoke concerning scripture. He would say, "you need to see it in the Word for yourselves." Nevertheless, years later, it became clear that so much of his teaching was out of context and rooted in fear. In hindsight, I remember the heavy sense of fear and judgement that was sprinkled within many of his teachings. Never-the-less, because I had no other frame of reference, I chose to ignore it.

The gospel is too good to be true good news. The yoke of Jesus is easy, and His burden is light. It's safe to pursue the grace of Christ wholeheartedly and without fear of judgment. Any and everything in our New Covenant that causes believers to be anxious, fearful and heavy is an out of context deception, unsupported by scripture.

An important second rule of Bible study that we'll rely upon throughout this work, is that we don't take one verse of scripture and run with it. "In the mouth of two or three witnesses, shall every word be established." God, the Father, spoke these words as recorded by Moses in the Old Covenant. Jesus, the Son, personally spoke the same thing as recorded by Matthew in his gospel account. And then finally, we have the apostle Paul, as led by Holy Spirit in the New Covenant, speaking these same words to the church at Corinth. Father, Son and Holy Spirit, in the mouths of Moses, Jesus and Paul all saying that we must have at least two voices in scriptural agreement saying the same thing, for a doctrinal foundation to be established.

Concerning this first component of the gospel, the forgiveness of sins, I hope to leave nothing undone. If we want to live free from guilt and condemnation with consistent confidence before our heavenly Father, it must first be established that we've been forgiven of our lifetime of sins.

Forgiveness is Past Tense

To have faith in anything pertaining to the Kingdom of God, it must be settled first that the focus of our faith has already been accomplished. In other words, if I'm believing God for healing, it must be settled first that provision for my healing has already been provided. Jesus took our sickness at the cross and today, "as He is so am I in this world." I don't have faith that I'm going to be healed. Right now, Jesus is whole, healthy, and strong. Because He's already been delivered from our sickness placed on Him, I too am healed in my body. This is what it means to fight from a position of victory, instead of fighting for victory. Right-believing faith is based on the truth of what Christ has already done. I am healed. As one patriarch of faith famously said: "God said it, I believe it and that settles it."

With this in mind, we know that a believer with faith in the gospel of Christ, doesn't wake up every day and ask God for healing. If we're believing God for healing, for example, we should be receiving Holy Communion from Jesus, in faith and with thanksgiving, that His Word is forever true. We would look back at the cross, examine our hearts for the full assurance of faith that we're completely forgiven and righteous in Him. Then we'd receive the benefit of His broken body and shed blood. To eat and drink in an unworthy manner would be to do so absent faith in the gospel, while struggling with guilt and condemnation for example.

In my humble opinion, Joseph Prince has the best book on receiving Holy Communion. It's entitled: "Eat your way to life and health."

How could it be that the weak are instructed by faith, to say "I'm strong," with courage and conviction? Or the sick to declare by faith "I'm healed," with praise and thanksgiving? But when sin takes place, religion instructs us to lay faith aside, remove the cross from the equation, and demonstrate before God, our doubt and unbelief. "Forgive me Lord, I've failed again." Is unbelief ever pleasing to God?

The scripture tells us that it's "impossible" to please God without faith. Yet, our religious traditions pertaining sin, instruct us to put on faithless remorse (like Old Covenant sackcloth and ashes) and confess the facts, not the truth. Please understand, there's absolutely nothing wrong with confessing our sin to the Father. We should be confessing our sins until we become free from a sin-consciousness. And that day will come. But we should confess our sins, not for the purpose of receiving forgiveness, but for the purpose of receiving help. God's desire is that we bring our cares and troubles to Him because He will always be the solution to every problem. But when we confess our sins to God, we do so in faith that we're already forgiven. We honor the work of the Son in full assurance of faith and from an altogether righteous position in Him.

In this next section, we're going to take our time and walk through the scriptures and hear the voices of many witnesses regarding the settled truth of our forgiveness. I would encourage the reader to take your time with this. When sin takes place and your faith is inevitably challenged, every believer should know where to go for comfort and strength. Through this process of building and strengthening our faith in the cross, sin also will become a thing of the past. Not that it won't take place anymore, but the rare instances of failure that penetrates our heart beyond the boundaries that we allow for ourselves, will be few and far between. A righteousness consciousness will become the ever-present new norm.

For many believers, this is the beginning of a transitional process. It's most important to place all our God-given faith in His Word, and not our experience. God has shown Himself willing to coddle us, as babies if needed, but He's after solidified faith.

Once and For All

Let's follow the first two rules of Bible study, allowing the Bible to interpret the Bible as we hear from two or more witnesses about what God has already done.

The Apostle Paul - Our first witness said:

> "In whom <u>we have redemption</u> through his blood, the <u>forgiveness of sins</u>, according to the riches of His grace." Ephesians 1:7

Redemption is freedom from the penalty and consequences of a binding agreement between two parties because the terms have been met. In this context, the debt for the price of sin has been paid by the debtor and accepted by the creditor. It means that believers are no longer held to comply with the Old Covenant of Law. This is a transaction that has already been completed. As a result, we (present tense) <u>have</u> redemption. Is Paul writing to an audience of believers that are living perfect, sin-free lives? Here's breaking news for some, that person doesn't exist. The people of the church at Ephesus over 2,000 years ago, are no different than the folks sitting next to you in church today. That includes the folks singing in the choir, greeting you at the door, and yes, teaching from the pulpit. Regardless of where you are or what you're doing, you <u>have</u> redemption right now, the forgiveness of sins.

In a letter to believers in a different city, Paul makes a similar statement, giving fresh insight into the details of this concluded transaction:

"And you, being dead in your sins… hath He <u>quickened</u> together with Him, having <u>forgiven</u> you <u>all</u> trespasses." Colossians 2:13

Very specifically, a trespass (sin) is a violation of the Law of Moses. Paul is telling us <u>all</u> trespasses against the Law have been paid in full. New Covenant <u>believers</u> are no longer under the Old Covenant, and therefore, <u>cannot</u> break the Law. Jesus paid this sin debt once and for all. The Law of Moses has no more hold against any New Covenant believer going forward. Paul also shares the reason why:

> *"For Christ is the end of the law for righteousness to everyone that <u>believeth</u>."*
> Romans 10:4

Believing in Christ and His work, liberates us from righteousness by our own works. However, New Covenant Christians can voluntarily place themselves "under" the Law, through unbelief. If we're under the Law were also under the curse of the Law. Notice also, "hath," "quickened" and "having forgiven you" are all clearly past tense.

The Apostle John - The next witness is the disciple "whom Jesus loved." In his old age at the end of his natural life, John shares this:

> *"I write unto you, little children, because your sins <u>are forgiven you</u> for his name's sake."*
> 1 John 2:12

Here we see that John is clearly addressing his spiritual children, born again believers. In agreement with Paul, John states that your sins are forgiven, past tense. John makes no mention regarding the behavior of his "children." He simply shares the benefit of the death of Christ at the cross. John also takes things further than you will hear in most churches. In 1 John chapter 3, He states that the New Covenant believer "cannot" sin. How is that possible?

You and every Christian you've ever known has committed sin. From God's perspective, we're dead to sin. Our entire covenant is based on this spiritual reality that religion refuses to embrace. We've been crucified with Christ regarding our former nature. The new man, the born-again man, the only part of you that God acknowledges, cannot sin because sin has been taken away and separated from us forever. Question: Is it possible for Holy Spirit to sin? The answer is that He cannot because He isn't under the Laws that governs man. Who is it that dwells in you???

This isn't to say that sin doesn't take place. But it is to say, as "new creatures" in Christ, we're to reckon ourselves dead to sin. Our "new man" is no longer under the laws that govern fallen man, by the same Holy Spirit.

Much like the movie "Weekend at Bernie's" though, we keep that old dead man alive by giving life and breath to the failures of sin. In the movie, the friends of dead Bernie put sunglasses on a corpse and drag it around, pretending it's alive so they can enjoy his wealth. We do the same thing by assuming the dead and crucified former self, has any standing before God.

The Apostle Peter - After sharing with believers the importance of adding to our faith, virtue, knowledge, temperance, patience, godliness, kindness, and love; Peter goes on to say:

> *"But he that lacketh these things is blind, and cannot see afar off, and <u>hath forgotten</u> that he <u>was purged</u> from his <u>old</u> sins."* 2 Peter 1:9

For the <u>believer</u>, the broad and wide path of destruction (not hell), but chaos in our lives, is the forgetting that we've been forgiven. When we lightly esteem this very important 1st component of the gospel, we choke out the benefits of the 2nd. And because the sins of our entire lives were forgiven over 2,000 years ago, they're all "old sins." Peter is warning us to keep the truth of our forgiveness of sins fresh in our mind, or we may lose sight of the very power that sustains us.

Many of us know friends and possibly family members that are born-again and confess Jesus as Lord, but their lives only reflect despair and defeat. This is a prime example of what Peter is saying here. When we lose the awareness of His forgiveness, or fail to become established in this truth, the same old habits and difficulties may return, if they ever left at all. Anyone of us could've fallen to such a state by simply neglecting "the faith," or by believing the lies of religion. There, but by the grace of God, go I. Notice again, "hath," "forgotten" and "purged" are all past tense.

The apostles, Paul, Peter and John are in full agreement that the New Covenant believer <u>has been</u> forgiven from all sin. These three witnesses seal the truth according to our second rule of Bible study. But God left nothing to chance.

John the Baptist - When John the Baptist saw Jesus approaching, He bellowed:

> *"...Behold, the Lamb of God, which taketh away the sin of the world."* John 1:29

Was Jesus successful in His assignment? We're saints today because we believed some time ago, that Jesus did exactly what John boldly declared. Sin is not our problem. The dismal results that we see in the Body of Christ worldwide, can be blamed entirely on a lack of faith in the gospel.

King David - And finally, the King and Priest after God's own heart, said this prophetically over 3,000 years ago:

> *"Blessed is he whose transgression is <u>forgiven</u>; whose sin is covered. Blessed is the man unto whom the Lord imputeth <u>not</u> iniquity..."*
> Psalms 32:1, 2

As we know, King David was not referring to Himself when He spoke these words. David's well-known adultery with Bathsheba and his role in her husband's death resulted in the death of David's son. The sin of King David was absolutely imputed to him, according to the Law of Moses. The King was speaking prophetically in this Old Covenant passage. Then, Paul repeated almost verbatim the kings' prophecy, saying:

> *"Blessed are they whose iniquities are <u>forgiven</u>, and whose sins are covered. Blessed is the man to whom the Lord <u>will not impute</u> sin."*
> Romans 4:7, 8

In quoting the king, Paul was confirming our present New Covenant reality. King David, before the cross prophetically, and the Apostle Paul afterward, are both in full agreement that the blessing of Christ's death is the forgiveness of our sins. Notice that even in the Old Covenant promise, David still wrote this future blessing in the past tense. Notice also that David and Paul both acknowledge the non-imputation of our sin because of the imputation of our sin upon Jesus at the cross.

> *"Blessed is the man to whom the Lord <u>will not</u> impute sin."*

The reason that the sin committed tomorrow, next week or next year will not be imputed to a believer, is because they've already been imputed to Jesus! God does not bow down to time, He created it. From outside the realm of time, He's declared that the sin that we've yet to commit, has already been imputed to Jesus. To take it a step further, God <u>cannot</u> impute your sin to you <u>and</u> Jesus, and still be just. It would be unjust for two to pay the sin-penalty of one.

From the moment we accepted Jesus as our Savior from sin, we received a full and complete reprieve from the penalty of every sin failure. Rest assured, the Word of God and His righteousness is unfailing and forever true. Our heavenly Father has not changed who He is, only how He responds to His children within the framework of this New Covenant. This is the love that God has shown toward each of us. Faith agrees with God and He is pleased. All our past sins have been forgiven. The proof is in the mouth of plenty of witnesses, as we've seen here.

In this first chapter, we have heard from witnesses two through seven; highlighted by God for our perfect clarity of Jesus' accomplishment at the cross: Paul,

Peter, John the Apostle, John the Baptist, and the prophecies of both King David and Jeremiah.

These are the sources (not exhaustive) that have been selected to confirm the finished work of Jesus for our forgiveness of sins. Now, let's hear from the first and best witness, the Master Himself.

Jesus - On the 3rd day after His death, His first day risen from the dead, Jesus Himself, implores us with this:

> *"Thus it is written, and thus it behooved Christ to suffer, and to rise from the dead the third day: And that <u>repentance</u> and <u>remission of sins</u> should be preached in His name among all nations, beginning at Jerusalem. And ye are witnesses of these things."* Luke 24:47

"Remission" of sins and forgiveness of sins, both come from the same Greek word aphesis. Remission is a more descriptive and powerful word than the more commonly used synonym "forgiveness." Remission is defined from the original Greek: "Freedom, pardon, deliverance, forgiveness, liberty; release from bondage or imprisonment. Pardon of sins; <u>letting them</u> (ALL) <u>go as if they had never been committed</u>." Jesus instructed the disciples to tell the world: In me, you're free from your lifetime of sin as if not one act of error ever occurred.

The word "repentance" is used by Christ to emphasize the line of demarcation between the Old Covenant and the New. Repentance here means to turn from an Old Covenant mentality of bondage, sacrifice, sorrow, and remorse to a heartfelt, faith-based appreciation for the pain, shame, suffering and death of our savior. Freedom in our thoughts from all the bondage of sin, instead of weighty, guilt-laden pleadings of "Forgive me Lord," is what repentance in our covenant looks like. No longer should we see God through the lens of our performance, but rather the performance of our Lord. This is the first step on the journey toward daily and perpetual confidence toward God. Every time a failure takes place, we have it within ourselves to release the "power of God unto salvation."

As we do, sin and sin-consciousness will lose all power and affect. The question that must be asked: Will you believe the scriptures in which your faith is founded?

Very few Christians have escaped the religious practice of pleading with God for forgiveness in every instance of failure, whether by an imposed religious tradition or in response to a guilty conscience. So, you probably have several questions. That's ok and in fact, good. My journey and every other escapee from religion and religious tradition began the same way.

I'm reminded of something that a former pastor once told his congregation years ago, which has proven to be profoundly true. He said, "if you want a lot of answers from God, ask a lot of questions." As we'll continue to see, the Holy Spirit will confirm the steps of your feet and the direction of your path by illuminating His Word along the way.

According to scripture, we've narrowed down the truth that there are only two components of the gospel, which together defines the grace of Christ. The forgiveness of sins is the first component of the gospel. The death of Jesus is the provision of God that deals with all our disobedience and every curse for all our sin. The cross represents the eternal solution for every evil thing that God has delivered us <u>from.</u> Full assurance of faith is only possible by fully embracing this work of God in the sacrifice of His Son.

Now, let's explore together the unsearchable riches of Christ made available to us through the 2nd component of the gospel, the gift of righteousness. The resurrection of Jesus is God's provision that assures us of all the promises, blessing, and inheritance that we are welcomed <u>into</u>, by Christ.

Deliverance <u>from</u> sin and <u>into</u> righteousness is what has been accomplished for us. The gospel is called the grace of Christ because there's nothing that we can do to earn, deserve, or merit the eternal love that God has shown toward us. Jesus did it all!

Confession of Faith

"I've been forgiven for every sin, disobedience and failure, once and for all."

I Need You to Trust...

You're forgiven of sin, it's no longer your problem

The blood of my Son is greater
than your lifetime of sin

Your sins and iniquities I remember no more

Your sin will never be imputed to you again

This gospel is forever settled in heaven

Righteousness with God

Righteousness with God

The Reward of Faith

The righteousness of God <u>in Christ</u> is forever settled in heaven. It cannot be changed, improved, or diminished. It's accepted, acceptable, and in fact, pleasing to God. The righteous perfection of Christ is the fulfillment of the Father's plan for salvation. The precisely executed assignment of Christ has earned Him an eternal reward of the highest honor at the right hand of God. His righteousness is what makes Him altogether lovely, without spot or wrinkle, holy, innocent, and undefiled. When we see the beauty and purity of the righteousness of God in Christ, we can better recognize the futility of trying to measure up in comparison. The gospel, or good news for the believer is that we don't have to. This is our covenant of the grace of Christ.

> *"For He hath made him to be sin for us, who knew no sin; that we might be made <u>the righteousness of God</u> in Him."* 2 Corinthians 5:21

I didn't do anything to earn it. I didn't do anything to deserve it. But I've been re-created perfectly and flawlessly righteous before God. In fact, I have the exact same righteousness as Christ Himself because it is His righteousness that I've been given. My life may not look like the life of Jesus, and I may not always say or do what Jesus would. Never-the-less, I'm <u>the righteousness of God</u> for one reason. I am <u>in</u> Christ.

By this truth and the blood that made it possible, I can approach the throne of God and simply hang out. I can spend time with Him talking, listening, or both. Nothing stands in the way of fellowship with my Father. Jesus' part in this work of <u>grace</u> is complete. Our part is determined by <u>faith</u> in His grace. By grace, through faith...

You have been set apart by God as well. He called you; sought you out, and you responded to His invitation. From the time that you said "yes, Lord," you became His and He became yours. You were born again with the Spirit of God, who took residence within your human spirit. And you both, became one. The angels of heaven rejoiced as God gave birth to a new child in the Kingdom of His Son. Your citizenship changed as well. From the kingdom of death and darkness to the eternal Kingdom of God. The proof is in the pudding. Do you have an inward witness of faith in Christ? If so, rest in this... the indwelling presence of Holy Spirit is your proof that you've received His perfect righteousness.

Every born-again believer is a child of God with right standing. The creator of heaven and earth is the one who has declared you righteous in His sight for all of eternity. Again, God's part is complete. He said it and then He did it. The only question that remains, do we believe? You may not look like it, and you may not feel like it either, but if you're a born-again believer, you're the righteousness of God...right now.

Regardless of your lifestyle, good or bad habits, personal quirks and idiosyncrasies, your status in Christ has provided you the privilege of confident and continual access to the throne of God. There are no good and bad children in the Kingdom. Only those in faith for His righteousness and those who have disqualified <u>themselves</u> from it. The difference is life, healing and hope, or defeat, despair, depression, stress, addiction etc. etc. The desire of the Father to impact every person on planet earth with His goodness is dependent upon this connection between our faith and His righteousness.

For the believer, the gift of righteousness is the primary blessing that affords us access to all others. Access to the Kingdom of God, our right-positioning within the Body of Christ, the inheritance of His peace and every other promise of God is dependent upon our understanding of this powerful endowment. With every revelation of His righteousness, our access widens; grace flows more freely, and our intimacy increases. It's no small wonder that Jesus instructed us to "seek first the Kingdom of God and <u>His</u> righteousness..."

Unfortunately, many believers interpret this to mean that we must begin "doing" like Jesus. This legalism trap of performance is common among well-meaning Christians. But what separates believers in Christ from every other religious group throughout planet earth's history is our righteousness with God has already been secured. Christians have nothing more to "do" to be righteous. We are to seek both, the resources of heaven, which manifest in our lives by <u>grace</u>, from an established position of <u>faith</u> in <u>Him</u> and <u>His</u> righteousness. By grace, through faith...

The path that our heavenly Father presents to every believer involves the surrendering of our noble aspirations to do good for righteousness and accept the good that's already been done on our behalf. Our good news forever, is the purity, holiness and perfection of Christ is freely offered to us for our daily bread. How much of His righteousness can you handle? Can you see yourself accepted in the beloved always, without your good or bad works playing a part? Can you see yourself flawless by the work of the flawless one? Seeking first, not our works of righteousness, but the gift of His righteousness, is true humility and an inherent challenge for every believer. The well-worth-it reward

Righteousness with God

for the overcomer is a life of restful confidence in our soon coming King.

Righteousness Lost & Found

In the garden of Eden, the first man created in the image and likeness of God was perfectly righteous. Adam and His creator enjoyed unrestricted fellowship with each other. He was blissfully ignorant regarding the knowledge of good and evil. He was naked, happy, guilt-free, shame-free, and confident toward God. Sin was not yet a thing. Righteousness with God didn't yet need to be defined in scripture because unrighteousness didn't exist. There was no need for faith because everything was abundantly supplied. Adam was well aware of the divine protection, provision and care that sustained him daily. This true and genuine righteousness with God afforded him the confidence and security of knowing that all was well in his world. But from the moment that Adam disobeyed God, death began to work in his body, soul, and spirit. Through his disobedience in eating from the tree that was forbidden, his pure and undefiled righteousness with God was lost forever. No one would ever again experience the same tangible righteousness of God as Adam, until Jesus.

All the scripture is dedicated to this one topic. Satan had legally penciled Himself into Adam's God-given authority in the earth, as the righteousness of God was forfeited. But, the plan of God to exalt His Son was already prepared. The task before God was to restore the righteous spirit, righteous soul, and the righteous body of His creation. Every aspect of mankind's fallen nature required a restorative solution. Freedom from all the curse of sin and death was God's objective for each of us. If God was to be successful in His original desire of fellowship with His creation, the plan had to be implemented to perfection.

This plan of God begins with something that never existed before. Throughout human history, righteousness-by-faith" <u>in Christ</u>, is the spiritual foundation for righteousness established by God to address Adam's fall. But before there ever could be a solution to the problem of sin caused by Adam in the garden, and before righteousness-by-faith could ever exist, the righteous one would have to complete the <u>work of righteousness.</u> Before the world was ever created, Jesus is the lamb slain from the foundation of the world.

Jesus is the righteousness of God personified. He's the perfect model of what righteousness says, thinks and does. In scripture, He's the "Righteous Branch" and "The Lord <u>our</u> Righteousness." Since before the cradle and beyond the grave, He's blameless, faultless, accepted and approved. Even as a child, He demonstrated His awareness of righteousness working in His life. At twelve years old, He instinctively knew that He must be, "about <u>my Father's</u> business." Over the next eighteen years, Jesus increased in wisdom, stature, and in (merited) favor with God and man.

Before He performed even one miracle, the Father personally declared, "This is my beloved Son, in whom I am well pleased."

The Father was well-aware that the full expression of His love and influence in the earth could flow through this perfectly righteous one. Through a developed understanding of righteousness with God, we can see in scripture that Jesus accessed the resources of the Kingdom of God at will.

After He entered the ministry at the age of thirty, Jesus performed miracles of healing, cast out devils, received supernatural provision and even raised the dead. He had no need to muster up faith for righteousness since childhood; it was all that He knew. He could rest in the comfort of knowing that the eyes of the Father were upon Him, and His ears were open to His cry. No one had more confidence to stand, fellowship and follow the Father than Jesus. When He prayed, He knew the answer was coming. When pressed to respond to a difficult question, He simply paused, anticipating direction from the Father. When challenged to confront a seemingly impossible circumstance, He restfully focused His heart on heaven, and saw what must be done. These acts are all demonstrations of the <u>Spirit of God</u> working through the <u>righteousness of God</u>.

Throughout the life of Jesus, He perfectly satisfied every demand for obedience and every promise for good success. He checked every box and left nothing undone. He performed every requirement and refrained from anything forbidden. *This beautiful demonstration of a life of purity, obedience and fulfillment of purpose is not modeled for us to be mimicked, but rather, to be received.* We've been offered a gift of credit for His sinless life and every act of His obedience. *God didn't demonstrate His righteousness for us so <u>we</u> can duplicate the works of Christ. He presented His righteousness for us to receive, so that <u>He</u> can duplicate the works of Christ, through us.*

As we receive by faith His righteousness, as the gift that it is, the Father is well pleased with each of us, individually. Before <u>God</u> performs any miraculous works through us; before we ever flow in the gifts of the

Spirit, or commit any acts of benevolent service, the Father is well-pleased with us as we honor His firstborn Son by living connected to His righteousness.

Since Adam's failure in the garden until the present, God has provided salvation through righteousness-by-faith in Christ. Prior to the cross, mankind looked forward in faith, to the eventual salvation that would be made available by Christ. After the cross, mankind looks back in faith, to the salvation package of benefits secured by Jesus' finished work. Every good thing that God has accomplished since Adam; every miraculous healing, deliverance, protection, or provision, in one way or another can be attributed to God, working through this vehicle that never existed before, righteousness by faith. Through the work of Christ at the cross, God has resolved every aspect of the curse of Adams disobedience.

Today, righteousness by faith in Christ is Gods supernatural solution and restoration plan for all of humanity. This is not the next best thing to the tangible righteousness-of-God enjoyed by Adam for a season. It's not less than; it's not second best, nor is it a consolation prize. It's God's own righteousness delivered to mankind a different way. Through faith in the integrity of God's Word, the gift of righteousness and the evidence of the indwelling Holy Spirit, we can live just as well-nourished, abundantly supplied, confident and free as Adam before the fall.

The Model of Faith

The introduction of righteousness by faith first began with God's selection of a man to best represent the simplicity of "the gospel." Abram was far from God in the sense that we think of righteousness today. His family and tribe were reputed to be worshipers of the sun, moon, and stars. In his day, there was no lawlessness because there was no law. Religious trespasses were a foreign concept because…

> "… until the law sin was in the world, but sin is not imputed when there is no law." Romans 5:13

Although Abram lied, committed adultery, and had failures of faith, God called him His friend. Every "thou shalt..." and "thou shalt not..." under the banner of the Ten commandments would not come for another 430 years. The only commandments that Abram had to live by throughout His life, was the voice of God.

Abram, whose name was changed by God to Abraham, considered to be the father of faith in the three predominant world "religions." The entire plan of God for man, after Adam's failure, was revealed in the following promises made to Abram. These seven promises are the blueprint from which the Kingdom of God on earth is being built today. Everything that God is doing in the world is centered squarely on these covenant promises made to Abram thousands of years ago. Even further, every other covenant promise that can be found in scripture are for the support of these seven. The key that unlocks most every door to understanding righteousness by faith, begins right here. These seven promises are made to Abram, *and his seed*.

Righteousness with God

While you read these scriptures, keep in mind that Jesus is the promised seed who will fulfill all. Jesus is the divine seed that will restore righteousness with God in the earth. God declared to Abram:

> 1) *I'm going to make of you a great nation*
> (a nation of kings and priests)
>
> 2) *I'm going to bless you*
> (heal, provide and protect you)
>
> 3) *I'm going to make you a blessing*
> (overflowing blessing that affects others)
>
> 4) *I'm going to make your name great*
> (the world is still talking about Abraham and Jesus)
>
> 5) *I'm going to bless those that bless you*
> (God will show favor to others who help us)
>
> 6) *I'm going to curse those that curse you*
> (others that come against you will regret it)
>
> 7) *In you, all the families of the earth are going to be blessed*
> (through Jesus, the body of Christ will bless the world) Genesis 12:2, 3

As you can see in the promises above, it seems that Abraham had no part or involvement in receiving this inheritance.

I count seven promises that God alone will do. This again, is pure grace. All by Himself, God is the "doer" of these promises.

The plan of God to restore the righteousness lost by Adam, required the faith of Abraham for a natural son. This, from a man and woman who couldn't bare their own children. If it was going to happen at all, it would be God alone who did it.

Abraham and Sarah had yearned for a male heir all their lives. The one thing that God needed and required of Abraham is the same thing that God needs and requires of us today. Agreement with God in what He's said and done is the believer's highest priority.

Abraham didn't believe what God was promising right away. According to scripture, it took about ten years before he could grab hold of what God was doing. First, he looked to make his servant Eliezer his appointed heir. Then God told Abraham the promise would come from his own bowels. That bit of information was badly misinterpreted by both, Sara and Abraham.

Considering Sara had been barren her entire life and was now in her eighties, she suggested that Abraham have sex with her mistress as a sensible option. It took God pointing out the stars in the sky and the sand on the shore, more than once, for Abraham to see the picture that God was painting. Finally, the scripture says:

> *"And he believed in the Lord; and he counted it to him for righteousness."* Genesis 15:6

A synonym for this word righteousness found in the Hebrew text of scripture is "Rectitude." I love this word because it makes clear the process and requirement of agreement with God. The best definition for rectitude, from Noah Webster's original 1828 Dictionary: "Exact conformity to truth."

Since the fall of Adam, it's not enough that God has declared something to be true. Conformity to that truth is necessary before God can bring it to pass. God walked with Abraham step-by-step, speaking along the way, until Abraham finally came to a place of rectitude. The reward for Abraham's faith was righteousness.

This newly acquired status of righteousness by faith is the exact conformity to truth that God needed to do the impossible.

Since the day that God made these promises, we see a very imperfect and flawed individual, perfectly delivered, supplied and protected. He received from God the manifestation of the promise, only after he came into agreement with God. This ought to help us better understand our own New Covenant. Jesus is the author and the finisher of our faith. In the example of Abraham, God initiated the plan. Then, Abraham believed God to the point of righteousness. And finally, little Isaac was born from the loins of a 100-year-old man and a 99-year-old woman. While the faith of Abraham was vitally important, it was God who started <u>and</u> finished the work.

Just as Abraham believed the covenant promises <u>unto righteousness</u>, before any "work" of God could be accomplished, we also must believe our covenant promises <u>unto righteousness</u> before we can experience confident and uninterrupted access to the Kingdom of

God. Those of us who have received salvation by Christ, must continue to believe the terms of our covenant:

> *"...For I will be merciful to their unrighteousness, and their sins and their iniquities will I remember no more."*
> Hebrews 8:12, Jeremiah 31:34

This is the perfect will of God for His children. He wants to write His will upon our heart and in our mind. He's the one who's declared, "I will be their God and they will be my people." Just like Abraham had to believe the promise of God for the manifestation of an <u>heir</u>, we must believe the promise of God for the manifestation of our <u>inheritance</u>. In both cases, the covenant terms and conditions for success were set by God. By faith in Christ and His sacrifice, God has brought the terms of our covenant within reach. It's His good pleasure to make us the "heirs of the world" with full access to all the promises of God in Christ. By the daily embrace of this gospel, nothing can stop the blessing of the Lord upon you!

Working the Works of God

Before we move on to even more good news, it should be made abundantly clear that righteousness with God is not a bad word. Many of us have received definitions of righteousness that prevent our ever attaining it. In and of yourself, you can never meet the gold standard of "Gods ways of doing and being right." Unfortunately, when the word righteousness is introduced, our instinctive reaction is to measure our character, morality, ethics, wisdom, and good decision-making ability, against that of Christ. Just an FYI, you will never measure up, and there's only heartache and pain in trying. Religion will

Righteousness with God

give you dozens of things to <u>do</u> to become accepted and well-pleasing to God. It cannot be stated directly enough, it's a fool's errand to try.

Consider the righteousness of Jesus in relation to God our Father. He was born into this world without sin. He perfectly obeyed every commandment and desire of God. On a scale of 1 – 100, His righteousness is clearly at the top of all seven billion of us presently in this world, and everyone that came before us. He's 100% righteous with the Father. Now, on that same scale, how would you rate your righteousness with God??? Please pause, consider and write your answer here: _____.

Do you consider yourself borderline unredeemable? Maybe you see yourself between 50-75% righteous. Maybe you stopped drinking, smoking, and have managed to avoid other old habits. Maybe you serve in the church, sing in the choir, are on the soul winning team at church and help build houses for single moms. Regardless of how far we've come, how chaste our lifestyle, or involvement in benevolent service to others, our own righteousness is putrid before God.

> *"But we are all as an unclean thing, and all our righteousnesses are as filthy rags..."*
> Isaiah 64:6

The sooner we embrace this truth, the quicker we can move in the direction of perfect freedom and pure righteousness with God. Not to be gross, but the scripture is saying here that our efforts and attempts at righteousness through our own works and achievements are like a soiled rag used for a woman's menstrual cycle, then offered up to God. "Look what I did Lord, how ya like me now?" Is not a good look. The scripture makes clear on several occasions the concept that God resists the proud but gives grace to the humble. When we try to earn, work for, or deserve His blessing (righteousness), we're bypassing His prescribed process. It shouldn't come as a surprise that He resists these attempts. Humility simply believes and says what God has already said and done. God honors our agreement with Him by guiding us deeper into His grace.

Righteousness with God

The God-ordained process that provides for increased fellowship in His presence and peace in every area of life, begins with hearing and believing the true grace of Christ. According to Jesus, the highest priority for every New Covenant believer isn't obedience to commandments or service to others. Hear what the Lord says is the most important "work" we can "do."

After feeding over 5,000 people by multiplying five loaves of bread and two fish in twelve baskets, with leftovers, the people were astonished. Some of them approached the Lord shortly after this to find out how they could be as awesome as Him, asking:

> *"What shall we <u>do</u>, that we might
> <u>work</u> the <u>works</u> of God?*
> John 6:28

Who can work the works of God other than God Himself? I'm certainly not qualified, are you? This is a legal question under the Law of Moses. Jesus usually responded to legal questions with legal answers, but this time was different. Jesus wanted <u>us</u> to have a clear and concise understanding. The motive behind "do," "work" and "works" is an Old Covenant mindset that began with the fall of Adam. Our human nature wants the credit, the sense of accomplishment, a reward for our effort and a pat on the back for a job well done. While there may not be anything wrong with these motivations in secular life, they don't work well with the grace of Christ.

God's influence in our lives cannot be earned or deserved, or it wouldn't be by grace. Instead of the high emphasis of "truly, truly" that Jesus would often say when He wanted to make an especially significant point, this time He went a step further. He included the question in His answer to insure perfect clarity:

"Jesus answered and said unto them, This is the <u>work</u> of God, that ye <u>believe</u> on Him whom He hath sent." John 6:29

What does it mean to believe on Him? According to Jesus, believing in the purpose and benefit of His death and resurrection is the "work" of God. Everything else is second to that.

Jesus is instructing us to learn and embrace this truth; by the work of God in Christ, we're completely forgiven. His righteousness became our righteousness the moment we accepted Jesus as our Savior. But since that day, we laid aside this first work of believing and replaced it with religious ideas of service. And of course, the best locator, where the rubber meets the road, is when sin of some sort takes place in our lives. If we truly believed that we're forgiven, we wouldn't deny our faith and seek more forgiveness. His work was perfect and complete. True and well-pleasing faith would thank God with gratitude and appreciation, that sin in every respect, has been completely and forever forgiven.

On the scale of righteousness with God in relation to Jesus, what number did you choose to best represent yourself? There's only one right answer. We are 100% as righteous as Jesus, freely. His perfect righteousness is offered to us daily. Credit for His lifetime of obedience, fulfillment of every Old Covenant commandment and perfect service to God is our reward for believing. To live in faith of this 100% righteousness with God all day, every day is our job. He's not after our <u>doing</u>, He's after our <u>believing</u>. If we can believe that we're 100% forgiven, only then can we live in the fullness of His 100% righteousness.

If you wrote a zero to best represent your righteousness with God, because you see your righteousness as gross as the earlier example, this also would be correct but not right. Your answer would reflect a sin-consciousness. Why would you defer to your old nature when asked a question about your righteousness with God? You have such a beautiful new nature. Our identity should default to the status of brand-new creatures in Christ instinctively. That old man is dead; he was crucified with Christ. Let's not count his righteousness as our own anymore.

And finally, any response between 1 and 99 reveals the full scope of everything from the lowest <u>unrighteousness</u> to the highest <u>self-righteousness</u>. All of which is the result of having heard and received mixed teaching. Can you do more good things to earn a higher position in relation to Christ? This is impossible. No, Jesus alone has made us perfectly righteous, and without Him, there's no righteousness with God to be found. What can we add to His shed blood and sacrifice to be more accepted by God? Any response less than 100% reveals how much more "work" in believing is necessary to rise above a performance-based Christianity.

The "work" of believing is present and ongoing. We all have family; friends, employers, preachers, what the scripture calls our "evil conscience," and Satan himself, all reminding us of how unrighteous we are. Before you even wake up out of bed in the morning, your flesh wants you to know how far you are from God. Nevertheless, we have Holy Spirit, the blood of Jesus and our own profession of faith, all on assignment to help our unbelief. Yes, study is involved in believing. Digging into the scriptures is a necessary part of the "work." But this primary focus of our faith accomplishes the "rectitude" that's necessary to establish a beautiful partnership consisting of <u>our</u> believing and <u>His</u> performing.

No matter what formula is presented to live a righteous, holy and purposeful life, there's only one gospel which activates the power of God unto salvation to get it done.

Breaking free from sin, rising above our natural circumstances, and finding confident intimacy with God, come by these words of Jesus alone. It's <u>His</u> grace, <u>His</u> power, <u>His</u> plan and <u>His</u> purpose that <u>He's</u> tasked to fulfill. Our job is to believe and keep on believing, step back and see the salvation of the Lord.

The Primary Assignment of Holy Spirit

As many New Covenant believers are aware, the Holy Spirit has been given to each of us for help and comfort in this life. It's Holy Spirit that moves upon us in times of worship and praise. And its Holy Spirit that leads us to the throne of the Father in prayer. He's a faithful and kind friend on assignment with the Father and the Son. The apostle Paul shares here, the shared heart of each person of the one, triune God:

Pure New Covenant Grace Series Part One

> *"The grace of the Lord <u>Jesus Christ</u>, and the love of <u>God</u>, and the communion of the <u>Holy Ghost</u>, be with you all."* 2 Corinthians 13:14

Christ is our salvation by grace through faith in His work at the cross. The Father is making every enemy of Christ His footstool, motivated by His love for each of us; and Holy Spirit is the one who makes fellowship with God possible. But there's a terrible myth about Holy Spirit that must be dispelled for the assurance of intimacy in a right relationship with Him.

Have you ever heard that the Holy Spirit "convicts" believers of sin? I sure have. In fact, I've heard it said many times in books, online and among family members and friends. But mostly I've heard it from the pulpit. I was told that the Holy Spirit reveals sin to us so we can repent. I was also told that this is how God corrects us so we can follow Him more closely. I just recently (2019) read an article from a popular Christian magazine that detailed 7 ways that the Holy Spirit convicts <u>the world</u> of sin. Included in this essay was the commonly accepted idea that Holy Spirit convicts' believers <u>and</u> unbelievers of sin. What could be wrong with that you say?

Righteousness with God

For whatever reason, these folks would have you to believe that Holy Spirit acts as an umpire, calling out sin in our lives. We know from scripture that Satan stands at the ready to whisper in our ear the facts of our failure at our most vulnerable moments. If both ideas are true, we shouldn't have any hope at all. How can we win the battle of sin in our flesh if God and Satan are working together? Of course, this is not the case at all. Just a bad interpretation of scripture passed down from generation to generation. The verse of scripture that's used to justify this can be found in the book of John as Jesus Himself, is addressing His disciples.

> *"Nevertheless, I tell you the truth; It is expedient for you that I go away: for if I go not away, the Comforter will not come unto you; but if I depart, I will send him unto you. And when he is come, he will reprove <u>the world of sin</u>, and <u>of righteousness</u>, and <u>of judgment</u>: Of sin, because <u>they</u> believe <u>not</u> on me; Of righteousness, because I go to my Father, and <u>ye</u> see me no more; Of judgment, because the prince of this world is judged." John 16:7-11*

In these verses of scripture, the Lord shares the work of Holy Spirit to three groupings that are in the world:

Pure New Covenant Grace Series Part One

1. Unbelievers 2. Believers 3. Satan

The word "reprove" from the original Greek text in scripture is defined: To convict, correct, chasten, chide, or admonish. So, Jesus is telling us the Holy Spirit is going to reprove the world: "Of sin, because <u>they</u>, believe not on me." Remember, Jesus is talking here to His disciples and directs His attention away from them, identifying His targeted audience as "they." The Holy Spirit is going to convict, correct, chasten, chide, or admonish those that "believe <u>not</u> on me." The primary assignment of Holy Spirit to <u>unbelievers</u> is the conviction of sin that prevents reconciliation to God.

Next, Jesus says the Holy Spirit is going to reprove those in the world: "of righteousness, because I go to my Father, and <u>ye (you)</u> see me no more." Here, Jesus turns His attention to His disciples. According to Jesus, the primary assignment of Holy Spirit to <u>you</u>, Christs' disciple, is to convict <u>you</u> of righteousness.

When you're feeling down, unrighteous, unholy, unqualified and undeserving of any good thing, the Holy Spirit is going to convict, chide, correct, admonish and chasten you, the believer. He's going to remind you

Righteousness with God

of the Word of God that you've <u>received</u>. He's going to emphatically persuade you of your righteousness in Christ! He's going to encourage and inspire you to embrace your righteous standing in Christ. Why? Because as Jesus said: "I go away, and you see me no more."

Our heavenly Father, Christ and Holy Spirit have been given a bad rap. Our "friend that sticks closer than a brother" has been poorly represented as a finger-pointer, that harps on our failures. Holy Spirit is not the one who nags, complains and rests heavy upon us when we sin. Nothing could be further from the truth.

When we finally embrace the gospel truth that we've been forgiven of all our sins and have accepted the righteousness of God as a gift, the Holy Spirit will be the first one to tell you to get up, brush yourself off and know that you are well-loved sons & daughters. He'll be the first one to remind you the sin debt has been paid by the blood of Jesus alone. He'll also assist with navigation, pointing the correct way to go in every situation as we lean upon Him, the one that knows all things.

The Work of Righteousness

"*And the work of righteousness shall be peace; and the effect of righteousness, quietness and assurance forever.*"
Isaiah 32:17

What does your best life look like? Can you imagine it as a completed 1,000-piece puzzle that together, reveals a beautiful portrait of righteous perfection? Now, pull a few puzzle pieces out for the hurts in your past. Remove a few more for the disappointments that you haven't let go of yet. Maybe a few more for damage done by your parents as a child. Let's not leave out the missing pieces created by religious teaching and false representations of God. Have you had a few bad relationships that's caused some emotional problems? Let's subtract a few more there. Is your bank account low? Is there sin in your life? Are there some health challenges? How's your career? Oh, my goodness! What happened to the beautiful portrait? No worries, it's still there, it's still yours. It's your best life, and only needs the righteousness of God to put all the pieces together.

According to the prophet Isaiah, when the grace of Christ is accepted and embraced, righteousness goes to work on your behalf. Apologies for this redundancy, but remember, righteousness with God only comes by faith, not by our good works of obedience nor by refraining from disobedience.

His righteousness doesn't need our help, only our faith. Not to be captain obvious, but a working righteousness makes all things right. As we fight the good fight of faith to stay connected to His righteousness, He's <u>working</u> to bring peace in every area of our lives.

Every emotional scar, painful childhood memory or experience; all shame and guilt, and anything that is incomplete in our health, finances, or relationships, are all deficiencies of peace. When righteousness is working, these missing puzzle pieces are approaching from nearby and far away. Some are coming in hot and fast and happen quickly. Others are seemingly coming in from a great distance and may take a little longer. But through a covenant promise <u>and</u> an oath, the "work of righteousness <u>shall be peace</u>."

Peace is what God Himself produces in the life of a believer who <u>receives</u> His righteousness. Shalom is the Hebrew word for peace. The greatest blessing that can be pronounced over someone is shalom because it encapsulates all that is good from God. From the Outline of Biblical Usage, Shalom - completeness (in number) complete safety, complete soundness, welfare, complete health, complete prosperity, complete quiet, tranquility, contentment, now watch this... complete friendship; of human relationship with God especially in covenant relationship. This is God's definition of the peace that we receive when we accept our covenant position of righteousness. Can you see the fearlessness that righteousness with God produces? He doesn't want us afraid; He wants us confidently intimate.

If ever there was a working model of Bible truth, the life of Jesus would be the masterpiece that best represents this verse. Since Jesus was born righteous with God, He only had to discover how this resource of righteousness worked. As we've seen, Jesus was well acquainted with His heavenly Father throughout His life. It's recorded in scripture that Jesus called God, "my Father" at the age of twelve.

In the four gospels, we see: "My Father," "Our Father," "Your Father," consistently throughout. How many times would you imagine that Jesus called on "Father" between the age of twelve until His ministry began at age thirty which wasn't recorded in scripture? His friends and family may have been a little jealous at times. But this is what righteousness looks like. It's a personal and intimate knowing that everything is good between you and God, as Jesus demonstrated.

Righteousness had been working in the life of Jesus for eighteen years prior to His ministry. By the time He was thirty, we can see the evidence that righteousness had perfected its work. Jesus had attained His promised shalom. No one can tell me that Jesus wasn't blessed in every area of His life; spirit, soul and body. It could not be that the righteous one didn't have shalom. No, everything was right and complete in His world as He prepared Himself to fulfill the call.

The first "effect" of righteousness, Isaiah states, is "quietness." To be tranquil, at peace, at rest and undisturbed. Carefree, anxiety-free, worry and stress-free living is the effect of "working" righteousness. How could Jesus sleep in a boat that was tossing and turning with high wind and waves? Righteousness was working. How could Jesus maneuver with ease around people who wanted His death above all else? Righteousness was working. How could Jesus provide the calm assurance of salvation to the thief who hung next to Him on the cross? Righteousness was working.

The next effect of working righteousness is "assurance forever." This word assurance, also from the

Hebrew text of scripture represents a place of refuge. This is a safe place because God knows exactly where you can be found. As kids, did you ever tie a string between two cans to create a homemade walkie talkie? When the cans and the string were pulled tight, you could clearly hear the voice coming from the other end. If that tight connection was maintained, there was unbroken communication. Living connected to the righteousness of God helps us to clearly hear every word of love, wisdom and instruction.

Great confidence is developed through this intimate communication as we hold fast to the gift of righteousness. When the wine ran low at a wedding, Jesus performed His first miracle. He heard from His heavenly Father and then boldly instructed the wedding crew to pour water into empty barrels. He didn't question Himself in fear, "what if this doesn't work?" He already knew what would happen. Remember also, when Jesus stepped out onto the open water, as if to say, "look what I can do?" All the healings, miracles, and provisions in the ministry of Christ were supplied supernaturally through working righteousness. No one has ever demonstrated greater assurance toward the Father than Jesus. With righteousness, peace, and confidence perfected, nothing was withheld from Him. Jesus proved that all things are possible through access to the Kingdom of God by righteousness. We have the same Spirit, the same access, and the same righteousness... by faith in this extraordinarily good news!

Every believer's first assignment is to believe the gospel <u>continually</u>, day by day. It's not enough that we believed yesterday. I'm sure we all want righteousness working in our lives every-day, along with the many benefits and promises afforded the righteous. Since every believer lives under a perpetual banner of forgiveness from God, every believer can also live under the banner of perpetual righteousness with God. Peace in every area is inevitable to the one who receives this working righteousness. Your best life begins now and will only continue until the perfect day.

Focus on the Good Side

My dad was a police officer in the city of Detroit from the sixties to the nineties. He was also an all-Navy boxer with mad skills. To me and my siblings, he was lighthearted and could break out in a song and dance at any moment. Our family and friends liked being around my dad because he knew how to keep things light and fun. But that was only one side of him. To those who would think to do us harm, he was fierce. As a kid, I once saw him punch a guy at a local gas station. For some reason, this man kept provoking my dad and even followed my brother and I outside of the station where the rest of the family was waiting. When this man refused to back off, persisting in his foolishness, my dad turned and punched this guy with a right cross that sent him flying in the air backwards. With the force that he was hit as he landed on the ground, he literally slid on his back and hit his head on a curb. It was like something from a Saturday morning cartoon. The only thing missing was the animated little birdies flying around this guy's head. We waited for the guy to regain consciousness before we left and hopefully no permanent damage was done. My dad was a superhero to me, but to that guy, he was a terror.

How we see God makes all the difference in the world. If we see Him through the lens of some of the Israelites under the Law of Moses, He's too loud, too hard, too big and too cruel. As we'll see in the next chapter, God's anger and wrath was a frequent response to rebels under the Old Covenant. But if we see Him through the lens of Jesus, He's patient, loving and kind. It's not that God is unpredictable or temperamental. He's always the same; reliable, consistent and faithful to respond to us, please listen to this clearly, according to the covenant that we choose. With our still-in-tact free choice, believers choose the limitations and boundaries of God's influence in our lives. Not only is it possible, but it's common for New Covenant believers to place themselves under the curse of the Law through unbelief. If I believe that I'm commanded to love God with all my heart, soul, strength and mind, I've placed myself under the terms of the Old Covenant. I'm inevitably going to fail and may be lured into fear of the consequences for my failure. On the other hand, I can choose to believe the motivation for love under the New Covenant. I love others, because God first loved me, as recorded in 1 John.

Everyone under the Law of Moses should be fearful of God. Under the Law, failure of obedience in one point is the same as if you broke every commandment. Every unbeliever, whether Jew or gentile, is also without excuse because of an inward knowing of right and wrong. Ultimately, everyone that has rejected the free gift of salvation from sin by Christ, must pay the price for their guilt under the Law themselves.

There's only one penalty for guilt, and the blood of an animal substitute is no longer accepted. So, whether someone has heard the gospel and rejected Christ, or have never heard the gospel at all, both will be judged according to the Law. In Paul's letter to the Romans, notice that each group of people have sinned, and both are going to be judged according to the strict standard of the Law of Moses.

"For as many as have sinned without law shall also perish without law: and as many as have sinned in the law shall be judged by the law..." Romans 2:12

Yes, God is seen as a terror by some, causing dread, panic and fright! But that's not for you or me! You're a New Covenant Son or Daughter! Regardless of your performance, God is patient and kind. Regardless of your behavior, He is forever merciful. All of God's anger, judgement and wrath for our disobedience was poured out on Jesus. There's none left for you. Hear what Isaiah prophetically reveals about the promise of God to His future family of believers:

"For this is as the waters of Noah unto me: for as I have sworn that the waters of Noah should no more go over the earth; so have I sworn that I would not be

Righteousness with God

wroth with thee, nor rebuke thee. For the mountains shall depart, and the hills be removed; but my kindness shall not depart from thee, neither shall the covenant (Abrahamic) of my peace be removed, saith the Lord that hath mercy on thee." Isaiah 54:9, 10

There's no reason to be afraid of God no matter what you've done, are doing or will do. God has sworn to never be angry toward you, and only show you loving kindness. Our covenant of peace with God is forever!

As Jesus came up out of the water from His baptism by John, the voice of God from heaven was heard.

"This is my beloved Son in whom I am well pleased."
Matthew 3:17

We, too, have been baptized into the family of God and granted eternal righteousness, just like Jesus. Therefore, we're not taking anything away from Jesus when we take this word for ourselves. Since He calls you son, you should say "yes, Dad or Father." Are you His favorite girl or any one of a billion? Despite what religionists will say, familiarity with God is a wonderful privilege of righteousness. I get great joy knowing that I'm so well-loved and pleasing to God, not by my works, but because of the acceptance of my position in Christ alone. Because His kindness will never depart from me, I can always run excitedly to Him, jump up on His lap, wrap my arms around His neck and give Him a big kiss on the cheek without fear or hesitation. I know that I'm welcome in His presence any time, day or night. And I never leave His presence in the same condition that I came.

I know that He sees and hears me because His Word tells me so. When I fall, He helps me up. When I win, He celebrates with me. He's the best Father a son or daughter can have. Righteousness tells me that this is the consistent quality and stability of our relationship, forever. There's never a time that I'm rejected or scorned, this too is His promise. There's never a time when His love is withdrawn or His attention somewhere else. This image of the Father is the same as the one provided by Jesus in scripture. I'm as approved of the Father as Jesus; I'm as pleasing to the Father as Jesus; and I'm as righteous as Jesus Himself. Those who say otherwise are struggling on the inside with the mixture of covenants. Haters and religionists will cry... BLASPHEMY! These are not my words but

Righteousness with God

Gods. And the reason that I can boldly make this claim is because it's His own and identical righteousness that I've received. I'm glad that God has a side to Him that causes men to tremble. I'm glad that He's seen as a fierce avenger to others, just like my natural dad. There's a lot of evil in this world, and I'm comforted in knowing that my Heavenly Father is patient and kind to me, rather than those who would seek to do me or my family harm. Each of us can rest in faith in His Pure New Covenant Grace, knowing that the Lion of the tribe of Judah is on our side.

Pure New Covenant Grace Series Part One

Paul's Warning to the Church

"*Now the Spirit speaketh expressly, that in the latter times some shall the depart from <u>the faith</u>, giving heed to seducing spirits, and doctrines of devils; <u>Speaking lies in hypocrisy</u>; having their <u>conscience seared with a hot iron</u>...*"
1 Timothy 4:1, 2

Today, many believers are under the false impression that sin is the biggest obstacle that prevents us from living a victorious life. The flesh also would agree with this prognosis, but it's not biblical. According to the gospel that Paul taught, wrote, and preached, sin is no match for the grace of Christ.

While sin is rampant inside and outside the modern church, the reason is clear. We must return to "the faith," which is the gospel. God has provided everything necessary for the Body of Christ to be the glorious church, right now. But the power of God unto salvation must be received to be lived.

For years I thought "some shall depart from the faith" meant that believers would turn their back on Christ, Christianity, and their place in the Kingdom of God. This is not the case at all. These blood-bought, spirit-filled, born again believers are in the church and love the Lord, but deny the gospel that got them there. <u>The faith</u> says we're forgiven and righteous by Christ. These believers have strayed from this original truth.

"Speaking lies in hypocrisy" is the pretense of representing something that isn't true. Noah Webster's 1828 Dictionary defines Hypocrisy: "Simulation; a feigning to be what one is not; or the assuming of a false appearance of virtue or religion; a deceitful show of a good character, in morals or religion; a counterfeiting of religion."

Notice that this hypocrisy is in direct relation to "The Faith." So, what is the pretense that is taking place in the modern church regarding the gospel of the Lord Jesus Christ? Acting, pretending, feigning to represent that one has received the forgiveness of sins. "I'm forgiven" <u>and</u> "Lord, please forgive me," is paramount hypocrisy. Those within the faith believe that they're forgiven and righteous with God. But those ensnared in the bondage of religion and hypocrisy have been seduced into thinking that the grace of Christ is somehow incomplete. Many believers have accepted the lie that their forgiveness is based on the blood of Jesus <u>and</u> their confession of sin. Still other believers think their righteousness is based on doing all right things. What can we add to the perfect work of Christ at the cross other than faith?

One moment we're deeply appreciative of the price that He paid for our sin as we reflect on our many errors. The next moment, we're seeking His forgiveness as if there was some sin omitted from the blood payment of Jesus. It's impossible to have been forgiven by God for all our sins and still require more forgiveness. I apologize for what may seem like an insult in this section. It's not. It's an awakening to righteousness, motivated by the Father's love for the purpose of blessing your socks off.

"Having their conscience seared with a hot iron...." Again, I mistakenly thought that this verse meant that sin was so prevalent and commonly accepted in the church, that these unfortunate believers could sin easily without guilt or remorse. On the surface, it seems like the scripture is addressing people whose conscience is dulled because of the repetitive practices of sin. But the opposite is true. These are born-again Christians with an acute awareness of sin. These believers have the markings of sin burned into their conscience, so they struggle with thoughts of guilt, fear, doubt, and judgment. These Greek words represent a branding of sin on the soul. Paul is describing people who have departed from believing that Christ died for all their sins and now live with guilt, condemnation, and a perpetual consciousness of sin. While this picture may be the extreme, there are varying degrees of this unbelief that's prevalent in the church today.

This used to be me. I confessed my sin, seeking forgiveness from God, even if I wasn't aware of any. I searched my heart daily for anything that would hinder my relationship with Him. I searched my heart again for sin before taking communion, as instructed. When I did fail in some area, things were worse. I'm reminded of one instance, driving down the road en route to serve God in a Sunday service, begging Him to stop my seed of sin from taking root. Barely able to see through tear-filled eyes, I was desperate to prevent a fictional harvest on my dirty deeds. Through the deception of religion, I had departed from the faith, gave heed to seducing spirits and doctrines of devils, spoke lies in hypocrisy and my conscience was definitively seared with the branding of sin.

I lived in that ungodly reality for far too many years. I was born again, Spirit-filled, generally happy and inspired, despite the bondage that I didn't know I was in. From the outside, you would've thought that this guy has it all together with God. On the inside, I thought I did too. I was welcome in His presence and excited to be there. My demeanor was upbeat and positive; I kept a song on my heart. But the guilt, shame and condemnation that originates specifically from unbelief, not sin, exposed the poor quality of my fruit.

Righteousness with God

Little did I know that God had something so much better.

Having successfully transitioned out of a lifestyle of unbelief into a daily faith in Christ, I can now say that I'm blissfully ignorant of the sin that I was once constantly reminded. I have no idea the last time sin took place in my life because it has no hold on me.

My fellowship, intimacy and confidence with the Lord is perpetual, like my sin-consciousness used to be. I'm righteous every-day, all day, for no other reason than the blood that made it possible. It's much easier to maintain a victorious position of righteousness by faith, than it is to try to be righteous by good behavior and works.

Paul admonishes us all, from our present position of victory:

> *"Stand fast therefore in the liberty wherewith Christ hath made us free, and be not entangled again with the yoke of bondage"* Galatians 5:1

Confession of Faith

*"I put on the new man, which after God
is created in righteousness
and true holiness."*
Ephesians 4:24

I Need You to Believe...

I will never hold sin against you because the
work of my Son has settled forever your
redemption and forgiveness

My Holy Spirit is always with you
to help you know and understand
who you are in Christ

He will bring to your remembrance every
right word spoken to your heart

I am always working in you,
perfecting every area of your life
through the gift of my righteousness

As you continue in the righteous
perfection of my Son, I will do great
and mighty works through you

The End of the Law

Pure New Covenant Grace Series Part One

A Tale of Two Trees

To best understand our present relationship with God, we must go back to the garden of Eden and look at creation from a fresh perspective. You may remember that God provided Adam and Eve access to all the trees of the garden. Although, two of these trees were especially significant. Adam and his new bride were both welcome to eat freely of the "Tree of Life." The fruit of this tree represents eternal righteousness with God, <u>by grace</u>. I define it as such because nothing had to be done to earn or deserve an eternal life of righteousness and peace with God. Plucking the fruit was all that was necessary to enjoy God's best.

Adam didn't have to qualify for the goodness of God; he had everything that he needed at His disposal. The result of eating from the Tree of Life would allow God to lead, guide and direct as He desired. God Himself, would be their personal instructor to assist in the navigation of a successful life. Raising their kids, working their jobs and interactions with each other would all benefit from intimacy and confidence with God through fellowship. There would be no measuring up to standards of performance, whether good or bad; only His gentle and kind leading on the various paths of life. Like kids in a candy store, the world was theirs to explore. This is the perfect will of God.

The "Tree of the Knowledge of Good and Evil," on the other hand was forbidden. Instead of having an acute sense of God, this tree produces an explicit sense of self. No one truly has a free will without the option to choose wrong. And so, God gave Adam a will of His own to choose as he pleased, with this warning: "for in the day that you eat thereof, you shall surely die." Adam eventually made the wrong decision. His conscience was opened to right and wrong, good works and bad.

"Self" became the center of his existence. The first thing that Adam recognized, after his disobedience to God's instruction, he was naked and afraid. A sin-consciousness and self-condemnation were already at work.

Eating from the fruit of this tree revealed to Adam, all that must be "done" to be accepted and pleasing to God. Adam's eyes were opened to a system of reward for meeting high spiritual standards (good works). From that moment, the knowledge of good could be used by Satan to push him into pride, arrogance, and conceit. The knowledge of other peoples "good" could also now provoke jealousy and envy. His newly discovered conscience either accused or excused his behavior. Self-righteousness through self-reliance, self-sufficiency, self-confidence, self, self, self was the new norm.

On the other hand, Adam would begin to sense all that was displeasing to God. With a clear view of the highest standard of expected obedience, failure to meet that standard brought all the pain that can be imagined. Any perceived fault or disobedience could now bring guilt, shame, condemnation and all the derivatives that come with them... i.e. fear, insecurity, anxiety, and stress. Adam traded in his own righteousness with God, which was good, acceptable, and care-free. In exchange, Adam would now taste of both, the discouragement and despair that comes with <u>unrighteousness</u>, along with all the pitfalls of fruitless <u>self-righteousness.</u> Judgement for failure either way could not be escaped.

This cycle of death began on the exact same day of Adam's disobedience, just as the Lord had warned. Satan now had a tool that he could use against Adam for every thought of obedience and disobedience. We can now see clearly why God forbade Adam from eating of this tree. This was our inheritance that we received from Adam at birth. Guilt, shame, condemnation, and death was never the plan of God for man. Going forward, He prevented Adam from eating the fruit of the Tree of Life to ensure mankind would not be trapped in this low-level living forever.

The Old Covenant is the tangible expression of Adam's disobedience in the garden. The Tree of the

Knowledge of Good and Evil has it's full and perfect expression in the Law of Moses. All the rules of do's and don'ts under the Law are the perfect <u>spiritual requirements</u> from God, for an imperfect and <u>carnal man</u>. Far from God's perfect will, God established the futility of pursuing a righteous status by doing good and rejecting evil. Today, the pursuit of righteousness any other way than the one that God has made, is the same hindrance to righteousness that it's always been. Righteousness with God was never possible through the self-efforts of an unrighteous man.

Righteousness-by-faith in Jesus is our intangible connection to the Tree of Life. God's plan to introduce a faith connection to His righteousness can be seen in the genealogy of Enoch, Noah, and Shem. Then the details of the plan of righteousness-by-faith was introduced by God to Abraham. This is God's strategy to restore righteousness and peace through fellowship with Him, to address every aspect of life that was lost through Adam's disobedience. Beginning with Abraham and concluding with the Son of God, the solution to all the curse that was unpackaged in the garden has been generously supplied. Nothing has been left undone.

These two covenants, the promise of God to Abraham and the demands of the Law to Moses, both sprung from the two trees in the Garden of Eden. These are the two options before all of mankind, throughout all of history. Righteousness-by-faith in Christ and His righteous perfection, or the inevitable failure of attempted righteousness with God through our own flawed works. Each of us have a choice to make every day. The path of the just is obedience <u>to the faith</u> which produces good works as a fruit. The path of the Law is obedience to do good works for acceptance and approval from God. Which tree are you eating from?

God's Plan A

Before the world was ever created, God saw the disobedience of Adam and the fateful plunge from his original position of righteousness. Adam disconnected from His source of life and power, he lost his glorious, God-like image and resemblance. This fall could have resulted in the upset of God's primary desire, which was open and intimate fellowship with His creation. Instead, God chose to salvage His creation project that Adam had almost ruined. With righteousness lost and fellowship tainted by guilt, fear and condemnation, God laid out His own strategy to revive both. The task before Him was clear;

He needed to re-establish man's connection to His life, power and influence by the restoration of righteousness. God's restoration Plan A, after the disobedience and fall of Adam, is found in the story of Abraham.

God's first objective was to identify a man willing to enter a covenant agreement with Him. A binding agreement between God and man affords God the legal right to intervene in the territory that was given to and lost by Adam. This formal agreement would establish an alternative route to righteousness, this time by faith. This man's willingness to agree with God would also become a model for God to demonstrate the path to righteousness for future generations.

After finding His man, God calls Abram (Abraham's name before God changed it), away from his family, friends, and the life that he had become familiar. He presented Abraham with 7 promises that would set the course for righteousness-by-faith. From before the creation of the world to our modern day and beyond, these promises are the words that God is watching over to perform.

The End of the Law

> God told Abraham:
>
> I will make of thee a great nation
> I will bless thee
> I will make thy name great
> You shalt be a blessing
> I will bless them that bless thee
> I will curse him that curses you
> In thee shall all the families of the earth be blessed

The first thing that we must consider are the identities of the two parties involved in this new path of divine supply by faith. We know that God the Father is one participant, but who is the other? The scripture makes this clear:

> "For when <u>God</u> made promise to Abraham, because He could swear by no greater, he swore by <u>Himself</u>..." Hebrews 6:13

Looking into the story found in the book of Genesis, we can see that God caused Abraham to fall into a heavy sleep. Leaving nothing to chance, <u>God the Father</u> entered this blood-covenant with <u>God the Son</u>... in Abraham. Therefore, this God-God covenant is perfect and full-proof because Abraham was only involved as a proxy for Jesus. There's no weak link in this covenant! To confirm this point, notice what God told Abraham here:

> *"I will establish my covenant between <u>me</u> and <u>thee</u> and <u>thy seed after thee</u> in their generations for an everlasting covenant, to be a God unto thee, and to thy seed after thee."* Genesis 17:7

Some have taken this term "and thy seed after thee" to mean the natural seed of Abraham, his twelve tribe descendants. But plainly, the Israelites are not a nation of kings and priests that best represent the Kingdom of God in the earth today. They're not representatives of the path to righteousness-by-faith, nor are all the families of the earth in process of being blessed because of them. There's no dual meaning for the term "seed" in the earth today. The scriptures interpret the scriptures, as always.

In the New Covenant, after the long-prophesied event of the death and resurrection of Christ, the apostle Paul provides this clarity:

> *"Now to Abraham and <u>his seed</u> were the promises made. He saith not, and to seeds, as of many; but as of one, and to thy seed, <u>which is Christ.</u>"* Galatians 3:16

The plan of God for restored fellowship with man through re-established righteousness would only be possible if Abraham had a <u>natural son</u> to be the carrier of a <u>supernatural seed</u>. Christ is that supernatural seed in the lineage of Abraham that would fulfill the Fathers strategy.

According to the seven promises that God made to Abraham that day, it appears like Abraham didn't have a role in the covenant at all. In these 7 promises, God shared what He would do all by Himself. But here's a critically important understanding that is relevant both then and now. Abraham had to believe that God was able to do something that was previously impossible. For a man who never had a child with his wife, and well past his prime, Abraham had to believe God for a son. From Genesis 15:6 the scripture says:

> *"And Abraham believed in the Lord: and God counted it to him for <u>righteousness</u>."*

This is the first mention of the word righteousness in the Bible and is crucial to understanding our own New Covenant. The same phrase that describes Abraham believing God unto righteousness, are repeated by Paul to the Romans, Galatians and his son in the faith, Titus. James also repeats it again to the twelve scattered tribes.

Believing God, not just regarding any random thing, but believing in... 1). The person of Jesus, and 2). His finished work, which then entitles us to... 3). All the promises of God under the banner of these seven.

These 7 promises all point to Jesus and His finished work. Well before the introduction of the Law of Moses, faith in the firstborn Son of God through these promises was the basis for God's influence in the earth. Every Old Testament exploit in scripture has been by grace (God protecting His plan), through faith in the Son and His finished work. Every time God invoked the names of Abraham, Isaac and Jacob in scripture, He was re-introducing His covenant plan of righteousness-by-faith. Jesus has been the center of God's divine strategy from the very beginning.

These 7 promises to Abraham are being fulfilled to the letter, through the death and resurrection of Christ. They're referred to twenty-four times in the New Testament as "the promise." After Jesus came out of the grave, He gave the disciples this direction:

> *"And, behold, I send <u>the promise</u> of my Father upon you: but tarry ye in the city of Jerusalem, until ye be endued with power from on high."*
> Luke 24:49

On the day of Pentecost, the Holy Spirit made His grand debut in the earth. He's been bringing the Father's plan to pass ever since. The Kingdom of God has been expanding daily as God began the building of His "great nation." The name of Jesus is spreading to every corner of the globe. Much has been accomplished, but much more is due.

From God's perspective, Jesus has completely restored everything that Adam lost in the garden on the day of His disobedience. In Christ, we have a New Covenant that reconnects us to His power and influence in our lives, through His own righteousness. By His finished work at the cross, we have confident fellowship with God, free from guilt, shame and condemnation. And finally, every promise of God that can be found in scripture are all a part of our inheritance under the banner of these 7 promises that God made to Abraham. We are the beneficiaries of all that Jesus has earned and deserves.

Righteousness-by-faith in Christ, is the one thing necessary to maintain an active connection to God's Plan A. This is the same today as it was over 4,000 years ago. As we awaken to the righteousness of God, our access to all the benefits of Abraham's infallible covenant promises between the Father and the Son are GUARANTEED!

Man's Plan B

Also, before the world began, as God beheld the full spectrum of time, He saw a "stiff-necked" and prideful people that wanted to make their own path and do things their own way. They wanted to be the doer of the work of God, rather than use the faith of God. This was the knowledge of good and evil in full effect. 430 years after God's Plan A was initiated through Abraham, God saw Abraham's descendants as unruly, unappreciative, and rebellious. To deal with them, God brought correction in the form of a covenant known as "The Law."

- The Law was given to a rebellious people who thought they knew better than God
- The Law was given to be a mirror for the people to see the reflection of their failure
- The Law was given to demonstrate the futility of righteousness by self-performance

God's desire for the Israelites was to show them that Plan A is the best and only option for success. Mankind would never attain the original posture of Adam, prior to eating from the forbidden tree, without doing things God's way. The fact that righteousness is an impossible accomplishment under the Law is underscored by Paul three times in this one verse of scripture:

> *"Knowing that a man is 1) not justified by the works of the law, but by the faith of Jesus Christ, even we have believed in Jesus Christ, that we might be justified by the faith of Christ, and 2) not by the works of the law: for 3) by the works of the law shall no flesh be justified."*
> *Galatians 2:16*

Paul couldn't have been clearer about how righteousness with God is NOT acquired. There's nothing that we can "do" to obtain the holy grail of righteousness with God.

The End of the Law

Below, Moses exposes a powerful truth concerning His covenant with God. He reveals that the covenant of The Law, is <u>in addition</u> to the promises of Abraham. The promises to Abraham and the Law of Moses have no relation. Unlike the God-God covenant of Abraham, Moses makes clear that his, is a covenant between God <u>and man</u>. Who's the weak link? Hear the words of Moses Himself:

> *"And Moses called all Israel, and said unto them, Hear, O Israel, the statutes and judgments which I speak in your ears this day, that ye may learn them, and keep, and do them...The Lord <u>made not</u> this covenant with <u>our fathers</u>, but with <u>us</u>, <u>even us</u>, who are all of <u>us</u> here alive this day."* Deuteronomy 5:1, 3

The reason that the Law was a failed covenant from the beginning is because a carnal, fallen, and unrighteous man cannot keep God's spiritual standard to obtain righteousness. This is underscored by Paul to the Romans:

> *"For we know that the law is spiritual: but I am carnal, sold under sin."* Romans 7:14

The truth of their carnality was especially so in the case of the Israelites after they came out of bondage to the Egyptians. Living in a heathen nation for 400 years will do that. So, the Law was given by Moses to teach a valuable lesson of the impossibility of a works-based righteousness. We still contend with that same carnal, fallen, and unrighteous nature as Paul. The Law was never offered by God for the purpose of fulfillment. It was offered to a people unwilling to submit to God's perfect Plan A.

> *"Wherefore then serveth the law? It was added because of transgressions, <u>till the seed should come</u> to whom the <u>promise</u> was made...*
> Galatians 3:19

The Law was designed as a temporary solution to a problem of wickedness. The date of its expiration is stamped on the day of your new birth in Christ. With every detail of God's plan fully open and naked before Him, God set out to work His masterpiece and created the world.

Co-Existing Covenants

From the day that the Law of Moses was introduced at Mount Sinai until the present, there have always been two primary paths presented by God. The promise of God to Abraham is the righteousness-by-faith covenant that runs high and horizontal, that links Abraham to Christ almost two thousand years later. Jesus is the fulfillment of the covenant promises of God to Abraham. On the other hand, the Law of Moses runs low, slow, and horizontal as well. It's designed to point to Jesus, and then having been fulfilled by Christ, made obsolete in the lives of believers.

Although these two covenants run parallel to each other, they're a great distance apart. Even still, the Law, the spirit of the Law, and the curse of the Law is still working in the lives of all who adhere to self-imposed religious standards. Our effectiveness in the Kingdom of God is determined by which path we follow.

> *"And this I say, that the covenant, that was confirmed before of God <u>in Christ</u>, the law, which was four hundred and thirty years after, cannot disannul, that it should make the promise of none effect.* Galatians 3:17

The apostle Paul confirms that the Law of Moses didn't nullify God's promise to Abraham. Meaning, the two covenants, one of promise and one of works are both presently active, in full force at the same time. The next thing that stands out here is the covenant of Abraham was confirmed "<u>in Christ</u>." As mentioned previously, the covenant promises to Abraham was an agreement between God the Father and God the Son. Jesus, long before His birth in Bethlehem, was present for the confirmation of the Abrahamic covenant.

Here we see two covenants running parallel to each other at the same time. One by promise to Abraham, who obtained righteousness by faith in God's promise alone. And a second, to Moses who represented an unholy, "stiff-necked" and "rebellious" people. All our Old Covenant bible heroes were able to reach up through faith to the higher covenant, out from under the Law to accomplish the miraculous.

In Hebrews 11, in what many believers have come to know as the "faith hall of fame," we see many of the patriarchs, who were clearly under the Law, being celebrated for their agreement with God in faith. These exceptional men and women rose above the Law of Moses and laid hold of the Abrahamic faith of God. The difference is a matter of the heart. One is working with God and the other is working for God. Our Father much prefers a partner that He can perform glorious works through, rather than an industrious slave.

Righteousness with God by faith in the promises to Abraham is the much higher and blessed covenant. The futile pursuit of righteousness by obedience to the Law of Moses is lower and based on the quality of one's own performance. Paul shared this insight for clarity:

> *"Christ is become of no effect unto you, whosoever of you are justified by the law; ye are fallen from grace."* Galatians 5:4

Believers are not fallen from the much higher place of grace because of sin or failure. When we seek approval of God, to be accepted and pleasing to Him through our works, either doing good or refraining from bad, we've fallen from our rightful and blessed place of grace. Christ being of no effect is the worst-case scenario for the believer. Under the low-level Law of works-righteousness, the unearned and unmerited favor of God is shut-off. Ineffectual prayers, some that go no higher than the ceiling, others that are only sporadically received and an ever-elusive inheritance is not the plan of God for you. But this is the sad reality for far too many believers that are sincerely <u>trying</u> to live a life that honors God. It bears repeating that the Law of Moses was holy and righteous but flawed, in the sense that it could not produce righteousness in man. It only reveals the inevitable conclusion that the righteousness of God and righteousness with God is impossible by our works. The Law of Moses represents a dead-end discovery of sin, self and death.

The End of the Law

While some believers will fight to remain under the bondage of the Law of Moses, they disqualify themselves from ever attaining their higher purpose, which can only be fulfilled by grace. It's every believer's choice to surrender to the understanding that we are not the hero of our story. We were dead, dying and separated from hope when Jesus redeemed us from death, hell, and the grave. Without Him, nothing of eternal substance will be accomplished in this life.

A People in Rebellion

Several generations after God cut His covenant with Abraham, his twelve tribe descendants disregarded the promises of God and found themselves serving others in a strange land. They were enslaved by the Egyptians for centuries because of their rebellion. Eventually, they adapted to the pagan rituals of their Egyptian slave masters. Despite this, God was still watching over the natural carriers of His divine seed. He was still watching over His perfect Plan A.

We're all familiar with the wondrous deliverance that God performed by the hand of Moses.

The End of the Law

But to get an idea of the wickedness of the Israelites, we can hear from God Himself. He provides this instruction to the people a<u>fter</u> He delivered them from captivity:

> *"And they shall <u>no more</u> offer their sacrifices unto <u>demons</u> unto whom they have gone a whoring."* Leviticus 17:7

God also told them:

> *"...Put away the gods which your fathers served on the other side of the flood, and in Egypt and serve ye the Lord."* Joshua 24:14

And again:

> *"But they rebelled against me and would not hearken unto me; they did not every man cast away the abominations of their eyes, neither did they forsake the idols of Egypt..."* Ezekiel 20:8

Far too many Christians are under the misguided presumption that the Law of Moses is the perfect will of God. Still today, many are under the false impression that holiness and righteousness with God can be found in the "doing" of the Law. It saddens me to see sincere-hearted Christians trying to keep the law with the flesh when they've been made free by the Spirit. Even worse, some believe that we've been given Holy Spirit by Jesus so we can successfully fulfill the Law of Moses. New Covenant believers don't use Jesus to satisfy Moses. This is spiritual adultery.

As we can see, the depravity and rebellion of the Israelites is the context in which the Law was introduced. The Law is the result of both, the curse initiated by Adam's disobedience in the garden, and the Israelites rejection of God's promises to Abraham.

With this understanding, we can see that the Law <u>was</u> the perfect will of God, but for the purpose of correcting a desperately wicked, disobedient, and rebellious people. Even at the end of Moses life, he still didn't have a favorable opinion of his own people, saying:

> *"For I know thy rebellion, and thy stiff neck: behold, while I am yet alive with you this day, ye have been rebellious against the Lord; and how much more after my death?*
> Deuteronomy 31:27

Mutiny on the Mountain

To understand with clarity the surrounding context that led up to the introduction of the Law of Moses, we must begin with the children of Israel moaning and crying (but not to God) under the heavy burden of servitude in Egypt. The Egyptians had made things extremely difficult for them and the people were feeling the weight of long, hard days and short nights. The scripture tells us:

> *"And God heard their groaning, and God remembered His covenant with Abraham, with Isaac, and with Jacob."* Exodus 2:24

God was watching over the Word of His Plan A to perform it. His desire was to re-introduce the promises that He made to Abraham. Through the ten plagues, God demonstrated His supremacy over the false gods of the Egyptians. He then delivered the Israelites beyond the Red Sea to dry ground. The journey to the land promised by God was underway. Having reached the base of Mount Sinai under the constant guidance and protection of God, the Lord revealed the simplicity of the details of His perfect and gracious plan to Moses:

> *"Now, therefore, if ye will <u>obey</u> my voice indeed, and <u>keep</u> my covenant, then ye shall be a peculiar treasure unto me above all people: for all the earth is mine: And ye shall be unto me a kingdom of priests, and a Holy nation. These are the words which thou shalt speak unto the children of Israel."* Exodus 19:5,6

Before the introduction of the Law, God gave Moses <u>two</u> instructions to relay to the Israelites: "<u>obey my voice</u>" and "<u>keep my covenant</u>." This word "obey" from the original Hebrew language means to hear, to listen, to pay attention, to consent or agree.

The End of the Law

The word "keep," also defined from the original Hebrew means to guard, keep watch, and protect. So, God gave Moses two instructions to listen and pay attention to His voice; and to keep watch over, guard, and protect His covenant. The purpose for God's instruction was to re-connect them with the promises to Abraham, by grace through faith. Notice, these instructions are both accomplished internally, within the heart and mind. Then, Moses takes the instructions to the Israelites.

> *"And Moses came and called for the elders of the people and laid before their faces all these words which the Lord commanded him. And all the people answered together, and said, All that the Lord hath spoken we will "do."* Exodus 19:7, 8

This word "do," from the original Hebrew, means to work, to make, to produce, to fashion or accomplish. The Israelites response does not reflect the terms of agreement that God had brought forth. They dismissed God's Plan A that only required their internal agreement and awareness. Instead, they introduced their own preferred terms of external "work," as a condition for their cooperation. Did God say anything about working, making or producing in His instruction?

The Israelites rejected the spirit of faith and opted for works instead. They wanted God to be the author, but to finish the work themselves. The vital component of faith, which is necessary for the plan of God for righteousness by faith, is absent in this equation. Their response to God was an existential threat to His plan of redemption for man. Their pre-occupation with self, left no room for God to be their God. <u>Doing</u>, in the sense that is offered here by the Israelites is a breach of the covenant of Abraham. But wait, it gets worse.

> "And Moses <u>returned the words of the people unto the Lord</u>. And the Lord said unto Moses, Lo, I come unto thee in a thick cloud, that the people may hear when I speak with thee and believe thee forever. And Moses <u>told the words of the people unto the Lord</u>." Exodus 19:9

What was the response to the two internal instructions of God to re-establish the covenant of Abraham? They told God, you just tell us what to do and we'll do it ourselves... TWICE!

The End of the Law

God told them to listen to His voice and watch over His covenant. They disregarded His voice and rejected His covenant. The very next word that God said to Moses was "GO," and it did not get any better from there. From that moment on, God began laying out the terms of "The Law." God warned them first with a never-before seen or heard death sentence for disobedience.

> *"...Thou shalt set bounds unto the people round about, saying, Take heed to yourselves, that ye go not up into the mount, or touch the border of it: whosoever toucheth the mount shall be surely put to death: There shall not an hand touch it, but he shall surely be stoned, or shot through; whether it be beast or man, it shall not live: Then, there came thunder, lightning, smoke and fire."*
> Exodus 19:12, 13

It gets even worse yet. God told Moses and the people to get ready for the 3rd day. It would be a sight, sound and experience they would not soon forget. There was thunder, lightning, a great earthquake, smoke, fire and a trumpet that for some reason, kept getting louder.

The scripture doesn't reveal who's blowing this trumpet, but it blew so "exceedingly loud" that all the people in the camp trembled with fear.

Can you imagine this terrifying scene? The people were freaking out at the change that took place between the gentle leading through the wilderness after their deliverance from Egypt, and their new harsh reality.

The Law of Moses that was introduced on Mount Sinai that day met the precise spiritual requirements of righteousness with God. If it were possible for the people to obtain righteousness through their own works, the Law of Moses would have done it. However, it was not possible because of their fallen nature. God never intended for righteousness with man to come by our works. Not then, not now, not ever. These twelve tribe descendants of Abraham received exactly what they thought they wanted, just like Adam in the garden. What they may not have considered though, is that a works-based system that's just, must also include spiritual consequences for failure.

Mission Impossible

I was at a bookstore recently with my wife. We were passing through to the mall when I had the idea to ask the manager a question about the store's inventory. I knew on the inside that the manager was born again by how she was conversing with her subordinate. As I engaged this kind daughter of God with my bookstore appropriate questions, I was pressed to get a little more personal. I asked her questions about some of her Christian practices, which she seemed delighted to discuss. I asked if she confessed her sins to be forgiven. She responded with a big smile, "every morning."

I then asked her if she believed that she needed to love God with all her heart, soul, strength, and mind. She responded transparently again, "yes, I do. And I fail every day. But I thank God for His grace."

I wish that this sister's belief system was the exception but it's more like the rule. She's clearly mixing her New Covenant faith with Old Covenant Law. Failure is the only possible result for anyone trying to please God with their behavior. This dear sister has accepted failure as her lot in Christian life and living. Her religious practices and belief are a prime example of the mixture that Pure New Covenant Grace seeks to remedy.

A Pharisee lawyer asked Jesus the question, "tempting Him, and saying, Master, which is the great commandment <u>in the Law</u>." The question is specifically regarding "the Law." This interaction is repeated in Mark and Luke's gospel, but not Johns. The Holy Spirit is telling us, in three of the gospels, that the first and greatest commandment "<u>under the Law</u>" is this:

The End of the Law

> *"Thou shalt love the Lord thy God with all thy heart, and with all thy soul, and with all thy mind. This is the first and great commandment."* Matthew 22:37, 38

Jesus' response to the lawyer originated in Deuteronomy 6, <u>under the Law</u> given to Moses. When we understand the distinctions of covenants and their purpose, we can see why this is the greatest commandment. This is God's first, greatest and most effective commandment to expose the impossibility of attempting to please Him with our performance. You will fail. The Law was not created for success. The tree of the knowledge of good and evil was forbidden so that you would not have to live a life of failure and the many consequences associated with it. The Law was doing its job in the life of this dear sister. In her own words, she's accepted failure as her cross to bear. But the Law is not for her, as Paul identifies here:

> *"Knowing this, that <u>the law is not made for a righteous man</u>, <u>but for</u> the lawless and disobedient, for the ungodly and for sinners, for unholy and profane, for murderers of fathers and murderers of mothers, for manslayers, For whoremongers, for them that defile themselves*

with mankind, for menstealers, for liars, for perjured persons..." 1 Timothy 9:10

You are the "<u>righteous man</u>" in this verse if you believe the gospel. You're the righteous man because you've accepted His forgiveness through Christ. Otherwise, you would fit in somewhere below the righteous man. The Law has nothing in common with faith. Paul, to the church at Galatia offers this instruction:

"...the Law is <u>not of faith</u>: but, the man that doeth them shall live in them." Galatians 3:12

The commandment to love God with everything you've got is the first and greatest command at the top of the list of things "not of faith." But remember, it's impossible to please God without faith. Therefore, it's impossible for New Covenant believers to please God by keeping the greatest Old Covenant Law. Did Jesus love God with all His heart, soul, strength, and mind, to your credit? If you believe so, you're qualified for the reward of His obedience. This is the faith that pleases God.

The End of the Law

If you cannot accept the truth of this, Paul warns, "the man that doeth them shall live in them." This describes the woman at the mall.

Although we have an inheritance of rest and peace through faith, there is no peace in failing God daily. With a big, genuine smile on her face, she has rejected the higher life of blessing, by faith in His righteousness. By trying to please God through impossible works-based righteousness, she opposes herself and the dreams in her heart. Just like Adam and the rebellious Israelites under Moses, she has chosen a hard and difficult path.

This deception runs deep because she's probably exercising faith for other things in her life. Maybe she's believing God for marital restoration, or perhaps healing for herself or a family member. Her failure to live up to the standards of the Law may create enough doubt in her own mind to prevent the manifestation of the things that she desires. God isn't obligated to perform anything under the Law because everyone under the Law is guilty. Has God obligated Himself to keep scriptural promises to the guilty and unrighteous?

Of course not, and those who have accepted this motive for loving God, disqualify themselves from a consistently working righteousness.

The direction of religious leaders to love God all day, every day and with everything that you have is blatantly hypocritical. I would never place that demand on my children. I don't suppose that you would either. In fact, no loving father would place such a burden on his kids. Do we know how to love our children better than God? Of course not! The scripture tells us that God is love. Love, by the biblical definition is patient and kind, giving and self-sacrificial. Doesn't God know how to best love His children? The answer is, of course He does. But in this demand of God, He was not talking to his children. He was commanding servants under the Law. You may say, well, I'm a servant of God also. And this would be correct but not complete. You're a son or daughter, who chooses with your own free will, to serve the living God.

Jesus is the firstborn in the family of God. After the resurrection, there were an additional eleven. On the day of Pentecost, there were another one-hundred-

The End of the Law

plus, and so on. The family of God began with Jesus, our firstborn big brother. It's a great hypocrisy of religion for any church leader to place the burden of loving God with all your heart, mind, soul and strength on others, but deny doing so with his own kids.

Our focus shouldn't be on how well we love God but rather on how well we receive His love. Unlike Old Covenant servants, New Covenant sons and daughters draw from the love of God and share His supply with others. The gospel of John is the only book of the gospels that the "greatest commandment" isn't recorded. Jesus Himself, spoke these words, <u>not</u> to an Old Covenant lawyer, but to His disciples, saying:

> *"This is my commandment, that ye love one another, <u>as I have loved you</u>."* John 15:12

Notice that the love of God is supplied first. By receiving this gospel, we'll receive so much more of His love. Then, we can love from our overflow by grace, as God intended.

John, "the disciple whom Jesus loved," also reveals our New Covenant motive for expressing love to God and others. After the resurrection of Christ, John shares the same sentiment as Jesus (two witnesses), saying simply:

"*We love Him, because He <u>first</u> loved us.*"1 John 4:19

My prayer for this sister at the mall and for you, is freedom from the bondage of every Old Covenant commandment that's already been fulfilled by Christ. Reigning in this life is dependent upon our embracing Christ's victory as our own. Believing God for anything by faith, while dragging the cumbersome and heavy weight of the Law is a most difficult task, and far too often, fruitless. Failure is not our lot in this life or the next. Let's expect together all the blessing and reward that Jesus has earned and deserves. We are the heirs of the world and joint heirs with Jesus. This ripe and ready inheritance is ours by grace that we receive through faith... in this gospel!

Don't Even Touch It

As you may recall, the Israelites who were led by Moses out of Egypt, rejected God's supernatural guidance and provision at the base of Mount Sinai. God wanted to pick up where the children of Israel left off 430 years prior, which began with the promises that He made to Abraham. Righteousness by faith in Christ is God's only solution to the disobedience of Adam. The Israelites chose instead to work their own plan for righteousness, which limited the influence and involvement of God. In effect, they were proposing a new agreement for righteousness, that didn't include the righteous savior.

As previously discussed, the Old Covenant is an agreement between God and man. That's not a good thing. Please be reminded that this is a failed covenant from the beginning because sinful man cannot uphold his end. The sin-stained blood of Adam that runs through the veins of men will never allow righteousness with God through natural man's spiritual limitations. The Old Covenant is God's way of proving to all mankind that righteousness with God is impossible, except through Christ. From the very moment that God witnessed the unity of the Israelites against His divine strategy for righteousness, preferring their own instead, God accepted their alternative plan and all the dire consequences that came with it. As you can see in the following text, the Law of Moses is nothing to be desired.

To be clear, if the forgiveness of sins is not a settled matter, we're still "working" under the Law for the righteousness of God that's been freely given. Any religious ritual or practice that we add to our faith for righteousness is a work under a system that has already been fulfilled. Faith in the Son is the faith that pleases the Father consistently and without fail. Otherwise, we're working under the system of the Law. Under the system of the Law of Moses, everyone is under the curse. Please hear from the Apostle Paul regarding this important truth:

> *"For as many as are of the works of the law are under the curse: for it is written, Cursed is every one that continueth not in all things which are written in the book of the law to do them."* Galatians 3:10

Let's take a final look at the warnings of God to stay far away from all religious works of the Law and rid our lives forever from all the curse that comes with that religious system. While not exhaustive, this should be ample motivation to root out any semblance of the Old Covenant of Law and legalism in our lives.

The Law of Moses is a covenant for servants, not Sons:

> *"Wherefore thou art no more a servant, but a son; and if a son, then an heir of God through Christ."*
> Galatians 4:7

No one under the Law was a child of God with one exception. Jesus was the only begotten Son. But then, after His death and resurrection, He became the firstborn of many brethren. Children have privileges that servants do not. The concept of the family of God begins with Christ. In every family, with plentiful sons and daughters, there are always those that accept and relish the love of the Father and those that are working for His love through their accomplishments and behavior. John had both, Peter and James beat in this respect. Take your position, like John, the disciple whom Jesus loved as younger brother or sister to Jesus and sons and daughters of a loving and kind Father.

> *"Behold, what manner of love the Father hath bestowed upon us, that we should be called the sons of God."* 1 John 3:1

The Law of Moses is never satisfied:

Even the sincerest believer, can never please God by his works. The story of a conversation between Jesus and the rich young man proves this point without dispute. The man asked Jesus:

> *"Good Master, what shall I do that I may inherit eternal life?"* Mark 10:17

Doing for eternal life is about you, not God. God wants to be the doer and wants us to be the believer. The man

The End of the Law

asked Jesus a question pertaining to the Law, so Jesus responded with an answer regarding the Law. Jesus gave him the Ten Commandments, to which the man responded:

> *"Master, all these have I observed from my youth."*
> Mark 10:20

The rich man shared that he's kept all the Law his entire life, which is quite impressive. Clearly, he prospered in his business affairs and became wealthy. Yet, he still has an inner conflict and lacks the assurance of peace with God.

> *"Then Jesus beholding him loved him, and said unto him, One thing thou lackest: go thy way, sell whatsoever thou hast, and give to the poor, and thou shalt have treasure in heaven... And he was sad at that saying and went away grieved: for he had great possessions."* Mark 10:21, 22

Folks have long said that this man was grieved because he was greedy and money had a hold of him. Personally, I don't know of anyone who wouldn't be grieved if the Lord asked you to sell everything you own. Under the Law, however, there's always at least one thing you lack. There's always at least one impossible obstacle to overcome. No matter how hard you try to do good and be good, the Law doesn't bend or meet you halfway. It's as rigid as the stone that it was written on. In the sight of God, you will always come up short in your attempts to please Him with your self-efforts.

The Law of Moses is the Ministry of Condemnation and Death:

"For if the ministration of condemnation be glory, much more doth the ministration of righteousness exceed in glory." 2 Corinthians 3:9

Under the New Covenant, the truth of no condemnation to those in Christ is settled in heaven forever. God is not condemned and Jesus did not come to bring condemnation. The Law, on the other hand, is the Ministry of Condemnation. According to the Spirit of God, condemnation and the Law of Moses are synonymous. If we're battling against guilt, shame, condemnation or even our own conscience, the Old Covenant Law is working in our lives. There's no escape for New Covenant believers that order their lives according to Old Covenant works. Jesus saved us from our sin, but we're delivered from guilt, shame and condemnation by faith in the gospel. It's the gospel that replaces the sin-consciousness inherited by Adam to a consciousness of God's righteousness in Christ.

In this same chapter, verse 7, the Law is also referred to as the ministration of death "written and engraven on stones. There's no mistaking this is a reference to the Ten Commandments. Without understanding this, you, like the rest of the world would be under the false impression that God wants you dead for your failures. Nothing could be further from the truth. But his should be the strongest motivation for every believer to root out all remnants of Old Covenant influence in our lives.

The Law of Moses literally kills!

> *"Who also hath made us able ministers of the New Testament; not of the letter, but of the spirit: for the letter killeth, but the spirit giveth life."*
> 2 Corinthians 3:7

That's twice now that the Spirit of God has identified the Law as a killer. Don't believe me. Believe God. Death, which is destruction in all its forms is due the guilty. Either we're New Covenant acquitted or Old Covenant guilty. Our only two choices are life by the

Spirit of faith in the grace of Christ or death through guilt and condemnation for our failures under the Old Covenant. No amount of guilt is good. There's no such thing as righteous, or godly guilt. Trying to abide by the letter of the Old Covenant kills. Of course, it's not the instruction itself that kills, it's the condemnation that follows the sin contained in the letter, absent the Spirit. As we'll see in a later chapter, condemnation is Satanic territory. It's his dominion. This is where he wants us all. Because he's been condemned, he wants as many people as possible to be condemned with him.

The Law of Moses prevents unwavering confidence toward God:

"For the law having a shadow of good things to come, and not the very image of the things, can never with those sacrifices which they offered year by year continually make the comers thereunto perfect. For then would they not have ceased to be offered? because that the worshippers once purged should have had no more conscience of sins. But in those sacrifices there is a remembrance again made of sins every year." Hebrews 10:1-3

The strategy of God for the children of Israel under the shadow of good things to come, was to keep them conscious of sin, at least once a year. This way, they would also keep their mind on the sacrifice, representing Jesus. Then, God could do big, wonderful things for them and be who He desires to be to them. But, they had no hope for perfection the way God defines it here, because of this conscience of sins.

The Law is designed to produce guilt and condemnation at every trespass against it, always pointing to Jesus. A New Covenant believer who's sincerely seeking to please God with his behavior is reduced to this same timidity and even cowardice before God. It's a difficult life to be judged by the Law for your failures, rather than faith in Christs' success. In our New and better covenant, we're not even supposed to have sin in our consciousness. By focusing on the perfect work of Jesus, rather than our sin and disobediences, we begin to meet the Father's definition for spiritual perfection. Freedom from a conscience of sin. Hebrews chapter 10 from above goes on to say:

"For by one offering he hath perfected forever them that are sanctified." Hebrews 10:14

The Law of Moses Prevents Our Inheritance of Peace:

"Peace I leave with you, my peace I give unto you: not as the world giveth, give I unto you. Let not your heart be troubled, neither let it be afraid." John 14:27

The peace that Jesus died to provide each and every one of us, is running from us instead of to us if we don't recognize the symptoms of wrongfully applied Old Covenant beliefs. Until we grab hold of the righteousness of God by faith in Christ alone, completeness of mind, completeness of health, completeness of welfare, fellowship, provision etc., are elusive at best. Under the Law, there's missing pieces and gaps in our believing that prevent our growth. Paul warns fellow believers along these same lines:

"Now I say, that the heir, as long as he is a child, differs nothing from a servant, though he be Lord of all..." Galatians 4:1

We have a huge inheritance. But as long as we have trouble discerning our place in the kingdom between Old Covenant servanthood and New Covenant sons and daughters, though we be lord of all, we cannot access the inheritance.

The End of the Law

If you're dealing with guilt, which is often accompanied by various shades of condemnation, it's time to come out and you now know how.

The Law of Moses prevents us from pleasing God:

"For if they which are of the law be heirs, faith is made void, and the promise made of none effect..."
Romans 4:14

The failure to release working faith displeases our heavenly Father because He can't be the loving dad that He desires because of our unbelief. Grace reigns through righteousness and there's no righteousness to be found in keeping the Law. Galatians 3:12 tells us that "the Law is not of faith..."Therefore, God is legally denied His desire of imposed goodness in the lives of believers who reject His way. Only through mercy and miraculous interventions can God intervene in the lives of those disobedient to the faith.

The Law of Moses reveals pending judgment:

"For whosoever shall keep the whole law, and yet offend in one point, he is guilty of all."
James 2:10

Under the Law, there are none righteous; this includes born again believers. Although God has declared us righteous by the gift, the package must be opened and received. Otherwise, there's no scriptural basis to receive the promises. There are no promises of God in all the scriptures to Christians. Check it out, not one. A Christian is not entitled to healing, provision, protection, or any other kingdom benefit. Never are we called "Christians" in scripture by God our Father, Christ, or Holy Spirit. The covenant promises of God are only to "the righteous." The righteous is the man or woman that has accepted the truth of their forgiveness and embraces their new identity in Christ as the righteousness of God.

The Law of Moses promotes self-effort which produces natural results:

The flesh, just like the Israelites at Mount Sinai, just wants direction from God. Then, it wants to go out and make it happen. This is the spirit of "do" behind the Law. Do, Do, Do, rather than Done, Done, Done, is the mantra of the Law. How do you know if you're performing under the Law? Check your motives. If you do things to be accepted or to be pleasing to God, you're working. If you're performing certain activities by command or demand, you're working.

What would happen if you didn't "do" some spiritually significant practice like tithing? Would you be uneasy and fearful that your financial situation would collapse? Would you fall into guilt and condemnation? Would you have "opened the door" to Satan and the curse of the Law? If so, you're working. This door will remain closed forever by simply staying connected to Jesus and His righteousness. I'm not recommending you quit tithing, only that you question your motives. Anything done with a works mentality is probably producing very little benefit.

Why we do what we do is an important question to ask ourselves. We're blessed because Jesus is blessed and we're in Him. Not because of Jesus and... (fill in the blank here). Begin today to identify areas of legalism and embrace the freely given power of God unto salvation.

The Law of Moses increases the power and effect of sin:

"The sting of death is sin; and the strength of sin is the law." 1 Corinthians 15:56

Although we've been delivered from the Law of sin and death, that sting will continue all our lives until we see Jesus more clearly. If you're struggling with sin, your real battle is not the sin but the belief system that you've erroneously received. Death lost its sting with the resurrection of Jesus. Eternal life with the Father is ours forever. Sin on the other hand reveals the absence of the power found only in the gospel. Those that place themselves under the Law through unbelief in the grace of Christ are feeding the old man, the old nature, the one who was justifiably crucified with Christ.

That man feeds on sin, guilt and condemnation. If we feed the old man and surrender to his will, he'll be much stronger than he should be allowed. This word "strength," from the Greek text, is the same as the word "power" that's used to describe the gospel. Either we surrender to faith in the power of the gospel, or by default, give in to the power of sin. By coming out from under the law of sin and death and continue in the grace of Christ, we weaken sin by starvation. This new lifestyle of faith in New Covenant grace will strip the power of sin's dominion.

The Law of Moses produces failure and denies us our God ordained position in Christ:

"Christ is become of no effect unto you, whosoever of you are justified by the law; ye are fallen from grace." Galatians 5:4

The difference between the Law of Moses and the grace of Christ is the difference between righteousness and unrighteousness, sons or servants, freedom, or bondage and even life or death. One is the perfect will of God. The other is forbidden fruit. Although Jesus was willing to humble Himself and take upon Him the form of a servant, He's far above and beyond Moses, in glory, identity, authority, power and honor. Today, He's at the right hand of God, exalted. Jesus represents the perfect will of God for man. Moses represents man's perfect will for man.

As we adapt to our secure position of righteousness in Christ, our inheritance with Him will not be held back any longer.

The Law of Moses limits the intimacy that God desires:

"God is faithful, by whom ye were called unto the fellowship of his Son Jesus Christ our Lord."
1 Corinthians 1:9

The greatest benefit of our salvation in Christ is fellowship in the seemingly tangible presence of God. The whole purpose for creation is to fellowship with the creator who has become our Father by the Spirit. Only by this gift of righteousness can we confidently, and regularly approach the throne of God. Only by the gift of God can we maneuver beyond the gates, passed the courts and get up close and personal with both, the Son and our Heavenly Father.

In His presence, only good can be found. Wisdom, healing, assurance, and fullness of joy is only the shortlist of benefits received from precious time with Him. This wonderful privilege afforded New Covenant sons and daughters should be taken advantage of more

The End of the Law

frequently than ever. Under the Old Covenant, nowhere is the presence of God available to man, with only one exception. The High Priest alone, could enter the Holy of Holies once a year to make atonement for the sins of the people. Even then, a rope with a bell was tied around his leg. If there was sin in his life, the priest would fall over dead. The sounding of the bell would signal his fate, and the other priests would drag the corpse out of the inner sanctum. If this were the case today, without the blood sacrifice, none of us would survive. This is another indisputable, irrefutable, and undeniable proof that God is not looking for sin in our lives, He's looking for faith in the grace of Christ. His presence is available to us as often as we desire.

Although the Law was spiritually perfect in every way, the height of its perfection could never be reached. Its primary objectives were to magnify sin, establish guilt and reflect the depths of pending judgment. Only then would the Israelites turn to His sacrificial solution that He's provided all along. Although the Law of Moses provided no hope for success in pleasing God through diligent obedience, merciful God still made a way of escape.

God orchestrated the system of animal sacrifice and substitution to prevent the death penalty from being applied to lawbreakers. When the Law was inevitably broken, the twelve tribe descendants of Abraham would look forward to their Day of Atonement to escape judgement. With every failure, they were reminded that blood would soon need to be shed on their behalf. Even though the Israelites rejected the plan of God for righteousness by faith in Christ, God still provided this model of hope for salvation by Christ. God was preparing the people for His Son, who would eventually be revealed.

Now we can see with clarity why God instructed the Israelites not to even touch the mountain at Sinai. Over 3,000 people died on the day the Law was introduced. With just a tiny measure of faith, this mountain can be removed, cast into the sea, never to be seen or heard of again.

A Final Word of Caution

Jesus, the person of grace adds to you like a trusted and valued friend; always supplying the spiritual necessities that feed and comfort. Of course, He's patient and kind, yet not soft; gentle and compassionate, yet not weak. He never raises His voice in anger or frustration. He's a perfect gentleman that doesn't push or demand. And He loves to lead us to good things on good paths as we follow His wonderful grace. He's a perfect representative of the Father, who is good, has good and does good.

The religionists, on the other hand, you know the ones, they like to snap their fingers at vulnerable servers, embarrass others from the pulpit, raise their voice against the brethren in anger, wielding their authority and ministry as if the power was their own, are steeped in the mixture of Old Covenant Law and New Covenant Grace. And while they place demands upon those that assist them, that may not look or sound like "Thus saith the Lord, thou shalt not do this or that," the spirit behind the words originate from a stony heart that has surrendered to the performance-based doctrine of the Law. Unlike a mean nun with a ruler at the ready to slap your hands for disobedience, these preachers and teachers make a far greater impact. The Lord once told me, "the greatest weapon formed against the church is the Law of Moses in the wrong hands." I understood what He meant, but never thought about it like that. It makes perfect sense. The enemy uses the failures of those under the Law to accuse the ones that are vulnerable to His accusations. What he's really after is self-imposed guilt and condemnation, as preachers and teachers use the Law unlawfully.

The End of the Law

If you're sitting in a service where the worship of the Lord is wonderfully blessed with the presence and power of God, but the ministry to believers that follows is burdensome and a weight on your soul, chances are great that you were just offered some Old Covenant leaven. If threats to believers of eternal separation from God are commonplace, that's the ministry of Moses, not Jesus, no matter how many times the name of the Lord is mentioned. If the ministry of the Word produces confusion and uncertainty concerning your future life with Christ, use your free will and run for the exits.

I'm reminded of the words of John once again, who shared this:

> *"The Law was given by Moses, but grace and truth came by Jesus Christ."* John 1:17

Please write this on your heart and mind that grace and truth are on the side of Jesus, not Moses. Holy Spirit only bears witness with the truth. As your walking out the course and plan of God for your life, it's not Holy Spirit who weighs you down along the way. While all of the Word of God is written for you, it's not all written to you. And there's a heavy price to pay for both, those who impose standards to qualify for God's goodness and blessing, and, for those who seek righteousness with God other than the way that He's made. There's no time like the present to transition out of the demands of the never-satisfied and ill-content, and into the steady and capable hands of grace.

    As I'm sure you remember, the Law of Moses was written on tablets of cold, hard stone. The Law is inflexible, rigid and makes no provision for failure. The New Covenant, on the other hand, is sealed with the warm and intentionally spilled blood of Jesus. Unfortunately, most believers are experiencing a combination of the two. The church at Laodicea is warned by Jesus Himself against mixing the cold with the hot. The warning from the Lord reveals His desire that whichever route to righteousness we choose, be committed 100%. Otherwise, there's very little to no benefit at all from either. Drawing from Old Covenant Law alone, at least has the God ordained purpose of driving you out, and fully into the waiting arms of New Covenant grace. Our present reality though, most churches and ministries are still attempting to fulfill the Old Covenant Law with the Spirit that came by the New Covenant blood of Jesus. While they're declaring the goodness of God in one breath, warnings of dire consequences for failing are shared in the next. Because there's just enough of the hot spilled blood that sealed our New Covenant fate mixed in with the rules, regs and judgments of Old Covenant Law, folks will return next week for more of the same.

Mixture by nature dilutes the purity of the final product. As it relates to the gospel, mixture waters down our power and kingdom effectiveness. Inner conflict, intermittent successes, mediocrity, and death is not the plan nor will of God. But this is the far too common reality for believers that have adapted to lukewarm provisions. Out of season apostles, prophets, evangelists, pastors, and teachers that demand obedience, submission, and service under the guise of pleasing a sometimes good, but sometimes wrathful God should be avoided at all costs. Even in the middle of this plandemic, it's important that believers not draw away from the local church. And what's even more important is that each individual settles into a church home where there are "able ministers of the New Testament," as Paul describes in 2 Corinthians 3:6. And while there is an awakening to righteousness taking place globally, right now, it's up to the global church to fall in line with the head of the church.

The familiar faces of family members and friends is not a good enough reason to continue some place where only a hint of His grace is present. What we're hearing is either proceeding from the throne of grace and shaping our lives under the New Covenant of grace and peace, or it's not. Jesus warned us against the dangers of receiving this mixture of covenants saying:

> *"...Take heed and beware of the leaven of the Pharisees and of the Sadducees."* Matthew 16:6

These words "take heed" is defined from the original Greek; to discern clearly, to perceive or see with the mind. If you can recognize the leaven, then you know exactly what to do with it. The leaven is self-righteousness. The Pharisees and the Sadducees were admonished by Christ for both, their desire to be exalted in the sight of men and their rigidly religious law keeping. Self is at the center of their pursuit of righteousness which disregards the effectiveness of the righteousness of God. Paul provides more insight into the nature of leaven to take over the whole, saying,

> *"A little leaven leaveneth the whole lump."*
> *Galatians 5:9*

Believers that are free and confident before God, but attend a ministry that is not, will soon adapt to the bondage or yoke of that ministry. Nothing slows one's progress towards liberty, or limits growth altogether, more than church doctrine that imputes rules and religious standards instead of the freedom that we have in Christ. Again, His power is contained within the rightly taught gospel. I won't take on the responsibility here for telling Christians to run as fast as you can from a ministry that mixes Old Covenant Commandments with New Covenant instructions. But apparently, the Apostle Paul doesn't have difficulty with it, stating:

> *"Stand fast therefore in the liberty wherewith Christ hath made us free and be not entangled again with the yoke of bondage."* Galatians 5:1

As we've seen, the yoke of bondage for the New Covenant believer is the Law of Moses. From the rooftops it should be proclaimed and made clear, all religious standards for righteousness must be removed from every area of our lives. As this occurs, we can see and hear more clearly the leading and guidance of Holy Spirit within. And as we fully embrace the finished work of our redemption in our past, we're free to run with Him and win the race ahead!

Life After the Resurrection

Pure New Covenant Grace is about making clear distinctions between life prior to Jesus' death at the cross and the resurrected life afterward. Prior to His death, every man and woman were under the Law of Moses. After His resurrection, everyone who believed on Jesus was free from the Law, and now under New Covenant grace. This explains why the first words of Jesus, on the first day that He appeared to the disciples, said this:

> "Thus it is written, and thus it behoved Christ to suffer, and to rise from the dead the third day: And that <u>repentance</u> and <u>remission</u> of sins

should be preached in his name among all nations, beginning at Jerusalem." Luke 24:47

Repentance from the mindset of works righteousness, by accepting the new relationship of righteousness by grace through faith, is the primary message of the cross. This is only possible through the acceptance of the <u>remission</u> of sins. He's not telling the disciples to be sorry or regretful, as we incorrectly use this word <u>repentance</u> today. He's not telling them to be remorseful or in sorrow. Jesus is introducing a new blood-bought system in relation to the Father. Faith in the remission of sins is how we access this new system's benefits.

This correct context helps us to best understand the words of Jesus in His two-fold assignment, prior to His death. Jesus was sent to overwhelm the failure of Adam and fulfill the God-Man Covenant of Moses. The Apostle Paul gives details of how Jesus would accomplish this task:

> *"Now we know that what things soever the law saith, it saith to them who are under the law: that every mouth may be stopped, <u>and all the world may become guilty before God.</u>"*

The End of the Law

>Romans 3:19

For God to free the entire world from the bondage of the Law, He first had to show them that they all had broken the Law. Only then would the people know of their need for a Savior. In other words, God exposed the guilty state of the whole world caused by original sin, to deliver us all from both, the sin and the guilt. Jesus would say things like: "whosoever looketh on a woman to lust after her hath committed adultery with her already in his heart." Mission accomplished there; all the men were guilty. Jesus also said: "whosoever is angry with his brother without a cause shall be in danger of the judgment (for murder)." Many believers are still under the impression that if they don't forgive others, they will not be forgiven. In revealing these, and many more Old Covenant standards, Jesus was raising the bar of the Law back to its original height of impossible perfection. He wasn't establishing a new religious standard for New Covenant believers to follow and embrace; He was establishing guilt under the Old Covenant. Like a tool in God's toolbox, the Law was used by Jesus to show us the depth of our fallen state so we would willingly surrender to His higher purpose of grace.

This use of the Law by Jesus was especially necessary for the religious order of the day. Through their oral traditions, they had watered down and lowered the Law so significantly that they all could keep it and claim righteousness. Rabbinical followers of Judaism had itemized the Law of Moses into 613 commandments. Supposedly, there were 248 positive commandments (do's) and 365 negative commandments (don'ts). For Jesus to deliver the world from this whole system of do's and don'ts, He had to function under the Law Himself. As God in the flesh, the sole representative of God, and the only man without the sin-stained blood of Adam, Jesus lived His life according to every do and every don't.

As the well-qualified, sinless, spotless, and wrinkle-free sacrifice for the sins of the world, the death of Jesus sealed shut forever, every qualification for righteousness-by-works. Today, faith in who He is and what He's done is the sole criteria for righteousness with God, and all the blessing, power and resources afforded to "the righteous."

Let's keep this important truth in mind. It's never the will of God to simply deliver us out of a bad situation. God desires to save us <u>from</u> an undesired status, and <u>into</u> a desirable status. Jesus didn't just deliver you <u>from</u> sin, guilt and condemnation at His death. He also delivered you <u>into</u> the blessing and promises of God through His resurrection. By faith in Him and His righteous perfection offered to you, as the free gift that it is, God has obligated Himself to make you an heir of the world. He's obligated Himself to use you to fulfill His seven promises that He made to Abraham in Genesis twelve.

Isaac, the son promised by God to Abraham, grew up to be a healthy and helpful young man. God asked Abraham to sacrifice this miracle son whom He loved. In faith that God would not allow his son of promise to be taken from him forever, Abraham followed the Lord's direction. Abraham led Isaac to the place of offering, intent on strict obedience. After reaching their destination, Abraham prepared his son for death.

He raised a knife high above his son, determined to plunge it into the chest of Isaac. And right at that moment, God stepped in:

> *"And the angel of the Lord called unto him out of heaven, and said, Abraham, Abraham..."*
> Genesis 22:11

This man Abraham was willing to do what God Himself had purposed in His own heart to do for us. Abraham had set the stage for the death and resurrection of Christ. This ultimate act of obedience moved God with compassion and prompted Him to take His promises to Abraham a step further. God told Abraham because he was willing to do this thing, in addition to the <u>promises</u>, He also <u>swore</u> that they would come to pass.

> *"Wherein God, willing more abundantly to shew unto the heirs of <u>promise</u> the immutability of his counsel, confirmed it by an <u>oath</u>: That by two immutable things, in which it was impossible for God to lie, we might have a strong consolation, who have fled for refuge to lay hold upon the hope set before us: Which hope we have as an anchor of the soul, both sure and stedfast..."*
> Hebrews 6:17-20

The End of the Law

By God's <u>promise</u> and an <u>oath</u> sealed in blood, your heavenly Father wants you to know that He's <u>obligated</u> Himself to bless your life through this self-imposed mandate. By faith in His Pure New Covenant Grace; that you haven't worked for and don't deserve, the forgiveness of sins and His righteous perfection in you, the blessing of God is inevitable. You couldn't stop your blessed inheritance if you tried. As we live connected to the righteous perfection of Christ by faith, and refuse to question the truth of your forgiveness, every promise of God in Christ is Yes and Amen!

From this moment on, when you fail, and guilt sets in, don't plead with God for forgiveness in unbelief and doubt. Thank Him for so loving you that He took all your sin and placed them upon Jesus at the cross. Thank Jesus for the pain, shame, suffering and death that He went through, all for you. Remind yourself who you are in Christ. And watch God honor your faith in the work of His Son with breakthrough after breakthrough, and from glory to glory.

Pure New Covenant Grace Series Part One

Now and forevermore, your heavenly Father will show Himself strong on your behalf as you honor Yeshua the Christ, the center of your joy!

The End of the Law

Confession of Faith

The Spirit of life in Christ Jesus hath made me
free from the Law of sin and death

I Need You to Know...

My work at the cross completely satisfied
all the requirements of the Law for you

I'm making fear and uncertainty a thing of the past

In me, you have perfect freedom

I have so much more for you as you transition
out of legal performances and into my grace

Your righteousness in me is as certain as my own

Where Do I Go from Here?

Thank you again for taking the time to read and absorb this material. I hope it was a tremendous blessing to you!

In Part Two of this Pure New Covenant Grace series, we're going to explore together The Greatest Deception. It's amazing that one verse of misapplied scripture has prohibited believers from receiving the abundance of the Grace of Christ. There are over a dozen reasons why 1 John 1:9 does NOT belong to the believer. This single scripture alone, used repeatedly out of context, is responsible for the great majority of unbelief in our

New Covenant. How the beautiful truth of 1 John 1:9 came to be misapplied to believers is surely a work of the enemy.

We're also going to look at, "Freedom From Sin." When we understand the truth about sin, all of the heaviness and self-doubt will dissipate into nothing. Sin and the effects of sin will no longer have any power over any of us. The cycle of sin, guilt, condemnation, repeat... will become a thing of the past. Freedom from sin will trigger a perpetual confidence toward God as Christ makes ready to present us blameless before the throne at His appearing. As we transition out of the mixture matrix and into the Pure New Covenant Grace of Christ, we'll see our Heavenly Father from a fresh, lively and active perspective. Intimacy with the Lord will come easy. Confusion will dissipate. Fellowship with God will be, like no other season of your life. Your love and appreciation for Him will continually increase as He reveals more and more of Himself.

And finally, we're going to explore and magnify how receiving the Love of God, which never fails, is the very practical, New Covenant way to receive an abundance of His grace. Grace to navigate through these times of uncertainty in the world will cause our lights to shine bright as we enjoy daily rest, peace and confidence by the knowledge of His love.

The gospel of the grace of Christ and the Love of God are synonymous. In order to approach the throne of grace with a much bigger cup and an expectation to receive an abundance of grace til that cup overflows, each of us must abide in our Father's love toward us. And there are no limits to how much of the love of God we can receive. As Daniel reveals prophetically concerning these present last days…. "They that know their God shall do exploits." I look forward to sharing the next installment in this 3 Part series.

Sincerest thanks,

David Branch, ETO

www.ingramcontent.com/pod-product-compliance
Lightning Source LLC
Chambersburg PA
CBHW021148160426
43194CB00007B/739